♦ THE FOUNDATION
PIECING LIBRARY ♦

QUICK AND
EASY QUILTING

THE FOUNDATION
◆ PIECING LIBRARY ◆

QUICK AND EASY QUILTING

More than 150 patterns
and inspiring Ideas for creating
beautiful quilt blocks

Jodie Davis and Linda Hampton Schiffer

Friedman Group

A *Friedman Group* BOOK

Library of Congress Cataloging-in-Publication Data available upon request.

ISBN 1-56799-950-6

Editors: Elizabeth Viscott Sullivan, Eleanor Levie,
and Francine Hornberger
Art Directors: Jeff Batzli and Lynne Yeamans
Designer: Tanya Ross-Hughes
Layout: Charles Donahue
Photography Director: Christopher C. Bain
Production: Ingrid McNamara
Illustrations by Barbara Hennig

Color separations by HBM Print Ltd.
Printed in Hong Kong by Midas Printing Limited

1 3 5 7 9 10 8 6 4 2

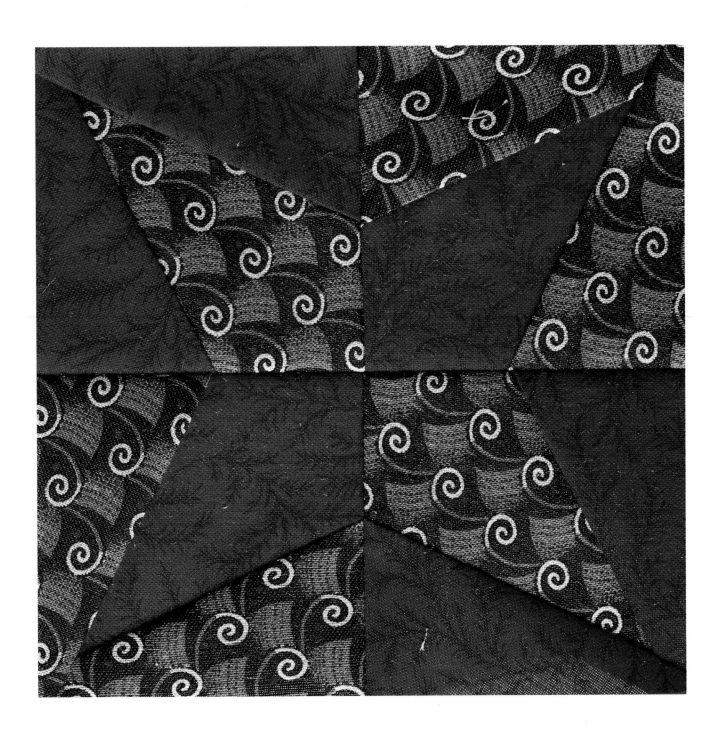

Contents

INTRODUCTION

WHAT IS FOUNDATION PIECING?

Foundation piecing is simply the fastest and by far the easiest method ever devised for constructing quilt blocks—so easy, in fact that even a complete beginner can make beautiful blocks. It's foolproof!

THE PROCESS IN A NUTSHELL

The blocks are constructed by machine sewing along lines drawn on a paper or fabric foundation. The foundation provides stability, the lines accuracy.

First, the block design is transferred to the foundation. With the marked lines face up, two pieces of fabric, right sides together, are placed under the foundation and stitched to the foundation

along the marked line. The two fabric pieces are pressed open, into place. More pieces are added until the block is complete. Finally, the blocks are sewn together, and voilá—a completed quilt top.

THE PATTERNS

The patterns included in this collection are based on Victorian motifs, garden imagery, and symbols of friendship and romance. Crazy quilts and log cabins, fruits and vegetables, hearts and flowers: all are combined in a potourri of wonderful block designs.

All of the block designs and quilting projects are rated for ease of construction, designated by the number of diamonds appearing on the page they first appear. If you are just beginning, select a pattern from those featuring one diamond. The most challenging patterns have three. The photographs of the blocks include their ¼" (6mm) seam allowances.

Foundation pieced blocks are the perfect opportunity for you to use those precious scraps of fabric you've been saving. And remember not to limit yourself to the block size offered in the book. Page 15 provides a chart to help you easily enlarge or reduce a block pattern.

THE QUILTS AND PROJECTS

More than twenty projects, each using one or more of the patterns from the Block Patterns section, are offered in the Quilt Design section. These will provide the perfect opportunity to put your new skills to use in creating a finished project.

What could be easier? No templates, no marking, no painstaking cutting. Foundation piecing is easy enough for a beginner, yet challenges the seasoned quilter. Above all, foundation piecing offers accuracy and speed. And it's fun!

JODIE DAVIS

PART ONE

FOUNDATION PIECING PRIMER

This chapter provides all the information you need to make the quilt blocks in this book. The only requirement is that you can sew along a straight, drawn line with your sewing machine. That's it!

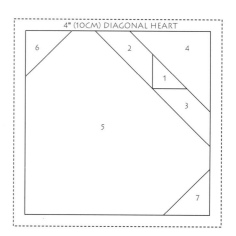

4" (10CM) DIAGONAL HEART

CALLING ALL HAND PIECERS

These patterns make excellent carry-along projects for trips, in waiting rooms, and after-school practice waits. Only a few sewing supplies and small scraps are needed.

For hand piecing, a fabric foundation is strongly recommended. Paper is too difficult to sew through by hand.

NOTE: You will be sewing from the wrong side of the blocks. The marked side of the foundation is the wrong side. For this reason the finished block will be a mirror image of the drawn designs in this book. Notice that for asymmetrical blocks, the photos of the blocks are in fact mirror images of the drawn block. For symmetrical blocks, there will be no difference between the drawn and sewn blocks.

THE DESIGNS

The block and border designs in this book are full-size, and all are ready to be traced and used. The numbers on the blocks indicate the sewing sequence for the fabric pieces.

The lines on the block designs represent the sewing lines. A dashed ¼" (6mm) seam allowance has been added all around the outside of each block.

Asymmetrical block

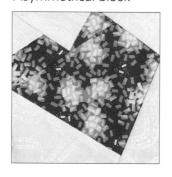
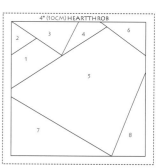

4" (10CM) HEARTTHROB

Symmetrical block

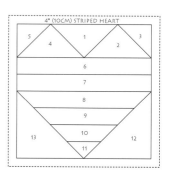

4" (10CM) STRIPED HEART

To make multiple copies of a block pattern on paper, transfer the pattern to a piece of paper. Lay this pattern on top of a stack of paper, perhaps ten or twelve pieces. With no thread in the needle of your sewing machine, stitch along the lines on the pattern. The holes will be your sewing markings.

FOUNDATION OPTIONS

Foundations can be either permanent or temporary, depending upon the desired end result or working method (hand versus machine).

PERMANENT FOUNDATIONS

A fabric foundation is permanent. The patchwork pieces are stitched to the base fabric, which is usually muslin. The foundation then becomes an additional layer in the quilt sandwich. A benefit for some projects (for instance, to add body to a wall hanging or vest), a fabric foundation isn't the best choice for others, such as a project calling for extensive hand quilting or a miniature that shouldn't be too stiff.

Choose good-quality muslin for your foundations, and be sure to prewash, especially if the finished project will be laundered.

NOTE: When using a fabric foundation, cut the foundation square with the grainline of the fabric.

CREATIVE OPTIONS: For exciting and unusual quilts, play with block orientation and combinations. Look at the patterns, their mirror (flipped) images, and combinations of both. Plan for the final block/quilt design that you want. To do this easily, use a photocopy machine to make several copies of the selected block pattern, then arrange and rearrange these blocks until you like the result.

I key my paper foundations for easier and faster piecing. By coloring in the sections (1, 2, 3...) according to the fabrics that go there, I eliminate confusion and speed up my piecing.
—Ellen Robinson, Germantown, MD

TEMPORARY FOUNDATIONS

Paper of many types is an excellent, inexpensive foundation. It provides more stability for piecing than muslin and eliminates the additional layer of a permanent fabric foundation, allowing for easier hand quilting. After construction, the paper is removed from the completed block by tearing. In some cases, this can cause fraying of seam allowances and distortion of the block; also, some bits of paper may remain stuck in the stitches. You can avoid these problems by using a shorter stitch length. This way, removing the paper will be similar to tearing postage stamps apart.

Leave the paper foundation in place until after you piece the blocks together. Blocks will be easier to align, and won't become distorted by tearing the paper away. This also eliminates concern about the grainline of the block edges.

Almost any paper is appropriate for foundation piecing. Copy, computer, and typing paper are readily obtainable. Available in grocery stores, freezer paper is favored by many quilters. The dull side of the paper is marked with the block pattern and the shiny side is pressed to fabric with a dry iron and a press cloth. Tracing paper has the advantage of lighter weight, so stitches won't distort as readily when the paper is torn away.

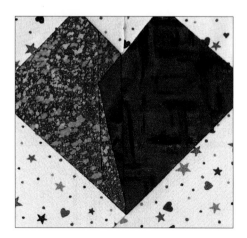

TRANSFERRING THE BLOCK DESIGNS

To reproduce the block designs on paper, trace or photocopy the desired pattern from this book. When tracing, use a ruler to ensure accuracy. Be sure to copy the piecing sequence numbers as well.

A copy machine makes quick work of reproducing patterns. To test the precision of the copies, make one copy of a block and measure to be sure the size is correct. Cut along the outside, dashed lines.

NOTE: If you use a photocopier to enlarge a block to another size, you'll need to redraw the seam allowance so that it's ¼" (6mm).

To transfer block designs to fabric, you may place the muslin over the block design on a light table or tape the design to a sunny window. Trace using permanent fabric tools. As an alternative, use heat transfer pens and pencils to speed the marking of fabric foundations. Following the manufacturer's instructions, make a transfer on paper and check it for accuracy. You can then make multiple replicas on fabric or paper using the same transfer.

NOTE: Be sure to use marking tools such as a pencil or permanent fabric pens when marking the fabric foundations. Pigma and Pilot SC-UF are good examples of the latter (see Sources). If the ink used is not stable it can bleed into the block front during construction or after the quilt is complete.

BLOCKS IN ANY SIZE

If you require block sizes other than those offered, start with the 4" (10cm) block and refer to the following chart to adjust the size; remember to adjust the seam allowances to ¼" (6mm) all around.

For a block size of:	Set the copy machine to:
2" (5cm)	50%
3" (7.5cm)	75%
5" (12.5cm)	125%
6" (15cm)	150%
8" (20cm)	200%

FABRICS

Fabric shops offer a delicious variety of fabrics for the quilter. High-quality all-cotton fabrics used in traditional quilting are a joy to work with and have a timeless appeal.

Many quilters are exploring the possibilities of such nontraditional fabrics as lamé, flannel, and unusual blends. For flimsy fabrics such as tissue lamé, fuse interfacing to the back of the fabric before use (tricot-backed lamés are preferred as they don't fray, nor do they require backing with interfacing). A muslin foundation will give thin, delicate fabrics the extra support they require.

PREPARING FABRICS

If you are using small scraps to make blocks, be sure each piece is at least ¾" (2cm) larger than the final patch dimensions. If in doubt, put the fabric against the back of the printed pattern and hold it up to the light.

For larger scraps or new yardage, cut strips at least ¾" (2cm) wider than the desired final patch. Or, cut strips 6" (15cm) wide for 4" (10cm) blocks; these can be cut into strips across the length to fit specific patch spaces as needed.

SEWING

For paper piecing set your sewing machine to 18 to 20 stitches per inch (2.5cm) or a stitch setting of 1½ depending upon the make of your machine. The short stitch length creates closely spaced perforations that will facilitate tearing away the paper, if that is your choice of foundation. Simultaneously, it stabilizes the seam.

Use an 80/12 needle. If you use a paper foundation, switch to a 90/14 needle if you have trouble tearing the paper away.

Choose your thread according to the fabrics selected. Light gray is a good choice for assorted lighter fabrics; dark gray for black prints and darker fabrics.

If you have trouble mentally flipping the image at first, carefully baste along each line on your chosen foundation *with no thread* in your machine using your longest stitch length. Now you will be able to see exactly where the seam will be, even when viewing the unprinted block face.

For final machine assembly of the quilt top use your normal stitch length.

When making multiple blocks of a pattern, Karen Kraft of Caledonia, MI constructs the blocks assembly-line fashion. She sews piece #1 for each block first, then piece #2 for every block, etc.

FOUNDATION PIECING METHOD

To demonstrate the foundation piecing method, I have chosen one of the easiest blocks in the book as an example. Follow these steps to make your own practice block.

REMEMBER: The marked side of the paper will be at the back of the finished block. Therefore, the finished block will be a mirror image of the drawn pattern.

> For smoother seams and fabric that's easier to handle, use spray sizing on your completed blocks before assembling them.
> —Ellen Robinson, Germantown, MD

> If you have trouble seeing the drawn line when sewing, switch to a clear or open toe foot on your sewing machine.

1. Starting with the shape marked #1 on the pattern, place the fabric you've chosen for piece #1 with the wrong side against the unmarked side of the foundation paper or fabric. Hold the foundation and fabric up to a light source to help you see the marked lines. Pin in place. Make sure the fabric covers the shape with at least ¼" (6mm) extending over the marked line all around. Be generous with the fabric: it's better to have too big a piece now than to come up short later.

2. Cut a piece of fabric for piece #2. Pin piece #2 against piece #1, right sides facing and adjacent edges even. Working from the marked back, stitch along the marked line; begin and end the stitching a few stitches beyond the ends of the line.

3. Trim the seam allowances to ¼" (6mm). For blocks 2" (5cm) square or smaller, trim to ⅛" (3mm).

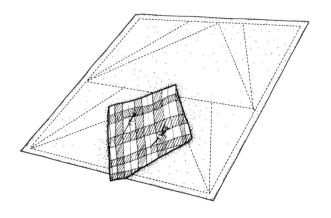

NOTE: Be careful not to cut the foundation when trimming seam allowances. Feel for the foundation with your fingers or scissors—or look. It will save you a lot of grief!

4. Fold piece #2 into place and finger press. Then press with a dry iron—no steam. In the same manner, add the third and all subsequent pieces, pressing as you go.

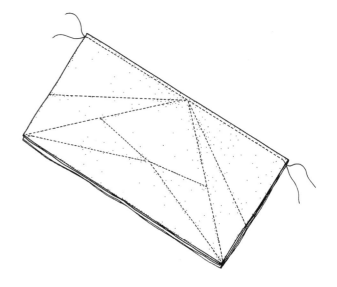

Instead of pinning the subunits together at the match points, try using vinyl-coated paper clips to hold the blocks together.

5. Using a rotary cutter and a ruler or square template, trim the edges of the block along the dashed lines. This leaves a ¼" (6mm) seam allowance all the way around the block.

OPTIONAL: Some quilters baste around the finished block from the right side, just inside the seam allowances. This anchors the fabric pieces so that they won't move out of place when you're joining the blocks.

SUBUNIT BLOCKS

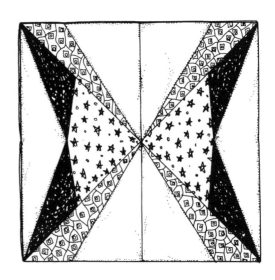

A few block designs consist of two (or more) pieces, such as two triangles or rectangles (subunits). The two subunits are prepared using foundation piecing techniques and then joined together to make a complete 4" (10cm) block, matching points and seams where necessary.

WHAT ABOUT THE GRAINLINE?

For all patchwork it is important to be aware of fabric grain considerations. Fabric is woven and you can easily see the intersecting threads, or grainlines. The lengthwise grain (parallel to the selvedges) has less "give" or elasticity than the crosswise (perpendicular to the selvedges) grain. If you pull a piece of fabric diagonally (at a 45-degree angle) to the grain, you will get a lot of stretching—this is the bias. When you assemble patchwork blocks, you should be aware that placing bias edges at the outside edges of the block will allow a block to stretch easily. The resulting variance of edge lengths will hinder easy joining of the blocks and prevent your quilt from hanging or laying straight.

One of the real virtues of foundation piecing is that this concern with grainline can be minimized. When using a permanent fabric foundation, be sure your pattern is applied to the foundation fabric even with the thread lines. Then you will not need to be concerned at all with the grainline of any of the patchwork fabrics you use to make your block. In addition, you can orient the printed pattern on your patch fabric to please your eye, with no concern for grain.

However, if you use a paper foundation and wish to remove the paper before final quilt assembly, you need to be careful not to put bias edges along the outer seam lines of your blocks. You can leave the paper foundations on the blocks until after assembly to alleviate this worry over outer bias edges. Be aware that paper removal can be tedious when working with a completed top. You may find a good pair of tweezers helpful in the paper removal task.

STITCH AND TUCK TRICK

Seven of the blocks (Playful Kitty, Ice Cream Sundae, Picnic Basket, Head Over Heels, Butterfly III, Love Bird, and Falling in Love) make use of a simple folding technique which allows you to negotiate a point without piecing.

Simply sew the seam as if it were straight, stop at the point with your needle down in the fabric and pivot, then continue on. Trim the seam allowances normally, then turn the fabric to the right side. Because you stitched the point, there will be a bit of extra fabric which you will then press into a pleat. If you wish, you may ladderstitch the fold of the pleat, though this is optional.

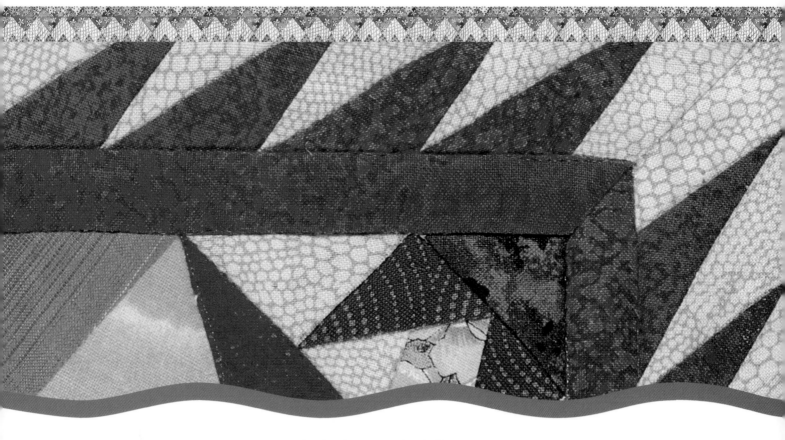

◆ PART TWO ◆
BLOCK PATTERNS

PATTERN COMMENTS

◆ = 1 diamond (easy)
◆◆ = 2 diamonds (modest difficulty)
◆◆◆ = 3 diamonds (challenging)

CRAZY PASSIONS

Perhaps inspired by an exhibit of traditional Japanese garments, the crazy patchwork fad swept the Victorian world. Many women enthusiastically embraced the chance to make an individualized work of art and show off their multiple needlework and quilting talents. These patterns offer a chance for modern quilters to further the tradition by experimenting with unusual fabrics and threads, rubber-stamped and photo-transferred images, hand inking, beading, and embroidery.

NOTE: All blocks are shown with ¼" (6mm) seam allowance.

BEGGAR BLOCK ◆

Confining the crazy patchwork within the body of this simple pattern allows you to use coordinating colors on the border. You can impose order and a "resting place" for the eye by choosing your corner fabrics carefully.

CRAZY PIECES ◆◆◆

Unlike most crazy patchwork, this pattern makes a recognizable design, in this case a whirling star. Four subunits make one block. Though this block requires more assembly than some patterns, the final effect is worth the extra work. Accentuate the star by choosing bright scraps for its blades and trailers.

These easy blocks were loosely based on four from an antique crazy patchwork quilt made around 1870 by Elizabeth Parkhurst Williams. You can see the striking original on page 147 of Kiracofe's *The American Quilt*.

CRAZY I, II, III, IV ◆

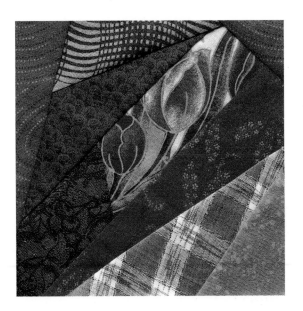

BEGGAR BLOCK

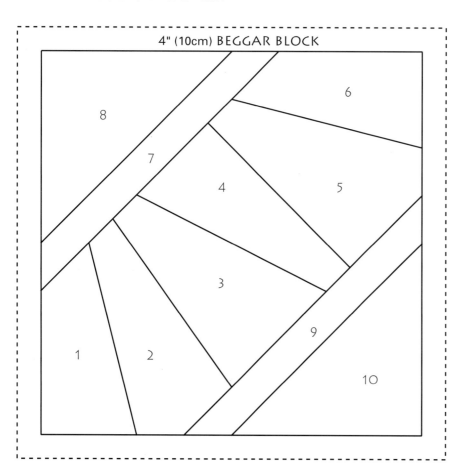

4" (10cm) BEGGAR BLOCK

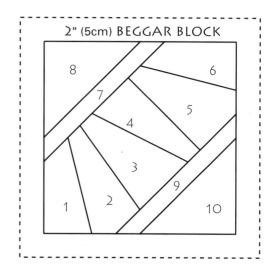

2" (5cm) BEGGAR BLOCK

Creative options

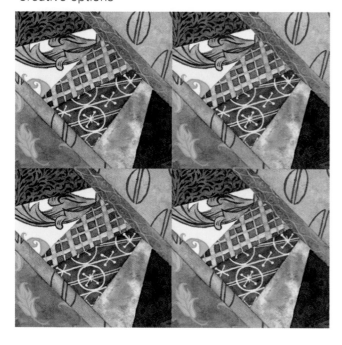

CRAZY PIECES

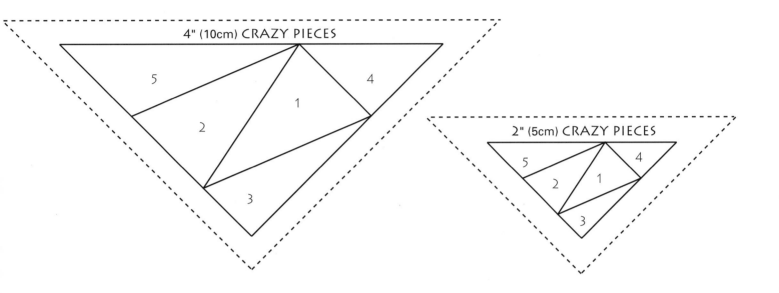

4" (10cm) CRAZY PIECES

2" (5cm) CRAZY PIECES

Creative option

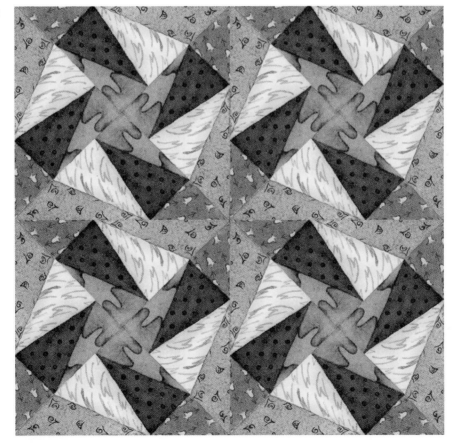

4" (10cm) CRAZY PATCH I

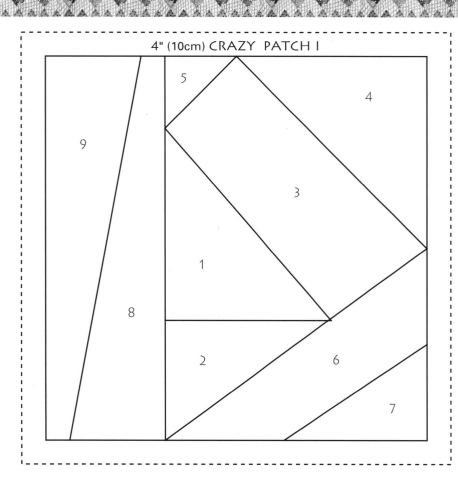

2" (5cm) CRAZY PATCH I

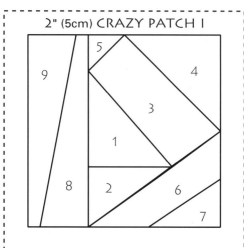

4" (10cm) CRAZY PATCH II

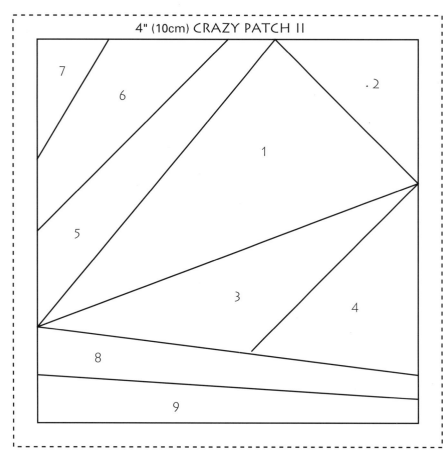

2" (5cm) CRAZY PATCH II

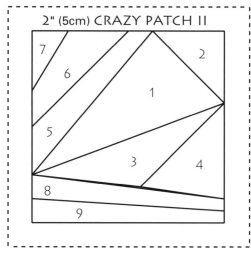

4" (10cm) CRAZY PATCH III

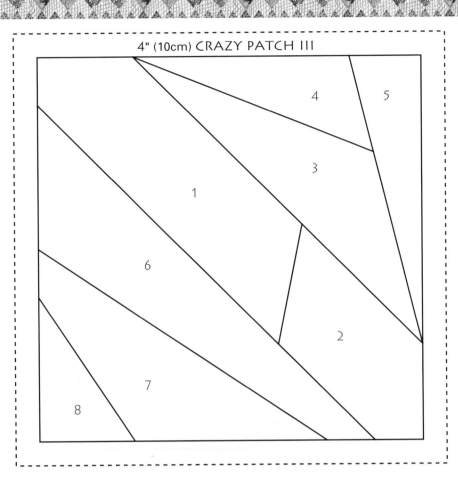

2" (5cm) CRAZY PATCH III

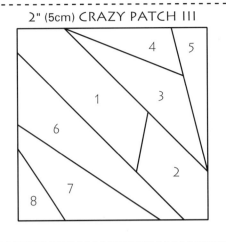

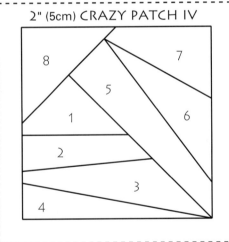

4" (10cm) CRAZY PATCH IV

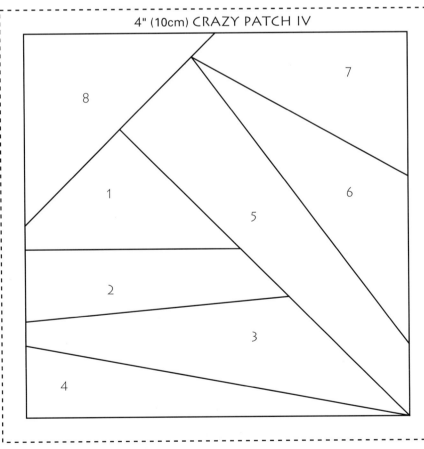

2" (5cm) CRAZY PATCH IV

ORIENTAL WONDER

Enjoy these blocks, whether you choose traditional Japanese indigo fabrics of contemporary Oriental prints. Or strike out in a different direction: wouldn't a fan design be lovely stitched from silk ties?

KIMONO ◆◆

This kimono has a bit more detail than most patterns, and so allows for more interest in the final "garment." A good pattern in which to feature those special fabric motifs you love, it requires subunit assembly.

CHINESE PUZZLE ◆◆

This traditional pattern will make a variety of interesting overall design layouts. Experiment! The assembly

of the two subunit pieces is very easy and requires no matching of points with the triangular block.

GENTLEMAN'S FAN ◆

This is an easy block of the "paddle" fan variety. Not overly feminine in shape, it can be dressed up or down depending on your fabric selection.

SAMURAI FAN ◆◆

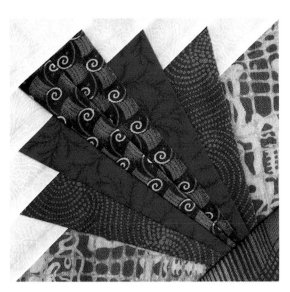

This block is actually very easy to do and requires no seam matching to assemble. You can choose very bold or traditional colors to make it striking. Corner triangles #8 and #9 are added after the two triangles are joined. Two subunits create one block.

MILADY'S FAN ◆

The folding fan was invented in Japan and was a part of every courtier's required costuming for centuries. We think of fans as a lady's accessory, useful for flirtation as well as decoration. This is an easy pattern to work despite its complex angles.

KIMONO

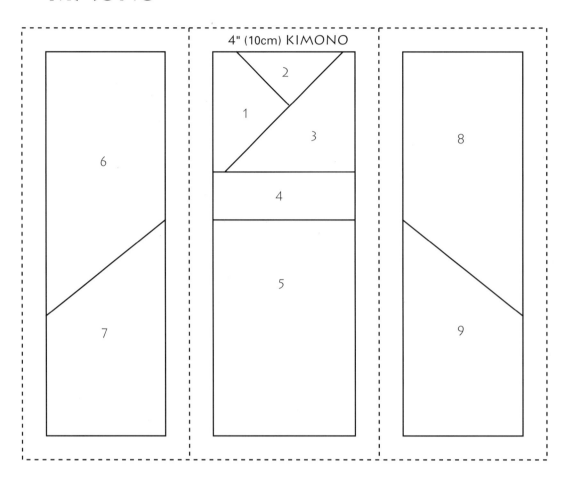

4" (10cm) KIMONO

Creative option

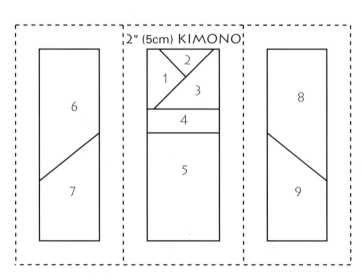

2" (5cm) KIMONO

CHINESE PUZZLE

4" (10cm) CHINESE PUZZLE

2" (5cm) CHINESE PUZZLE

Creative options

GENTLEMAN'S FAN

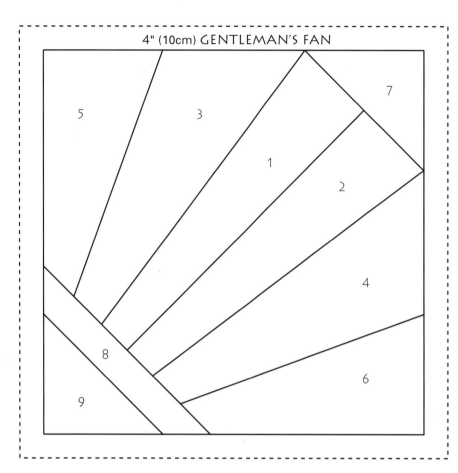

4" (10cm) GENTLEMAN'S FAN

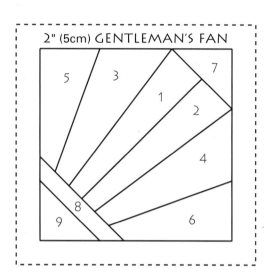

2" (5cm) GENTLEMAN'S FAN

Creative options

SAMURAI FAN

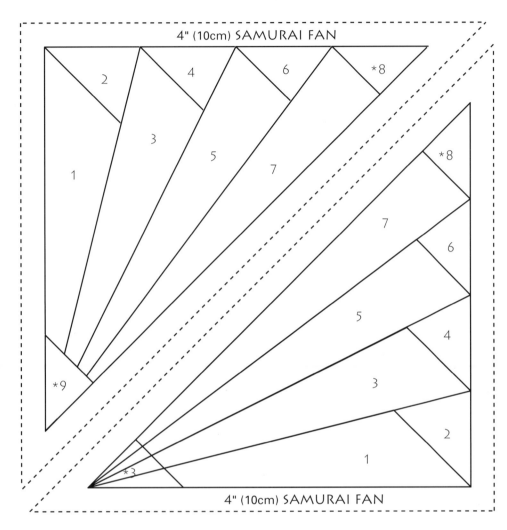

4" (10cm) SAMURAI FAN

4" (10cm) SAMURAI FAN

Creative option

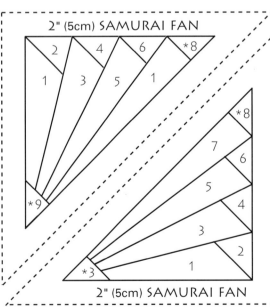

2" (5cm) SAMURAI FAN

2" (5cm) SAMURAI FAN

MILADY'S FAN

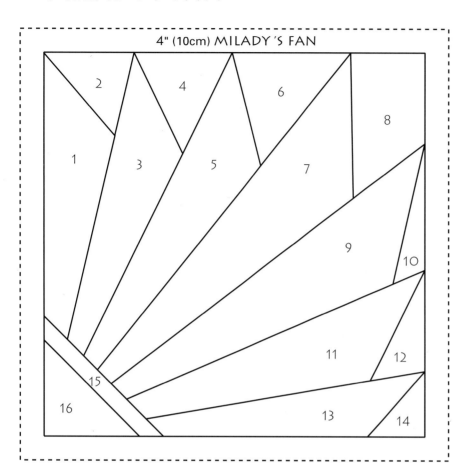

4" (10cm) MILADY'S FAN

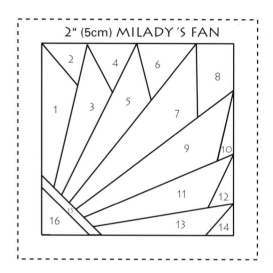

2" (5cm) MILADY'S FAN

Creative option

FRONT PARLOR FANCY

This assortment of patterns represents those found on "good" quilts, which were saved for "show." Enjoy making these and be proud to exhibit your resulting works of art.

ROSEBUD ◆◆

First published by the Ladies Art Circle in the late 1890s, this pattern can make interesting overall designs. It requires four subunits to produce one block, but there are no matching points to worry over until you join the blocks.

PALM FROND ◆◆◆

A three-leaved variant of a favorite traditional block, this pattern was first published in 1901 by the Ladies Art Circle. Four subunits make one block. Though challenging, it can be used for many interesting optical effects. Be sure to experiment with mirror images and various block layout combinations.

CROSS AND CROWN ◆◆

This is a variant of a favored traditional pattern, first published by Ladies Art Circle around 1889. Choose different center "sash" fabrics for spice.

PINEBURR BEAUTY ◆◆◆

This block is slightly more challenging as it requires matching points to assemble the subunits. Four sub-units make one block. Look carefully at your choice of background fabrics if you decide on an overall block layout—you can achieve some exciting contemporary effects.

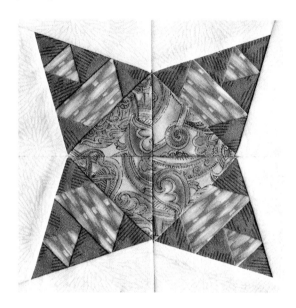

CROCUS ◆

This very easy flower pattern is homage to the many beloved red, white, and green floral quilts made in the last century. Careful shade choices of fabrics for the petals will give depth to the blossom.

DELECTABLE MOUNTAINS ◆

Delectable Mountains has been a favorite patchwork pattern for more than a hundred years, appealing to old-time traditional quilters and contemporary fabric

artists alike. Here, the tedious "feather" points have been reduced to an easy foundation block. Experiment with different block layouts; many variations exist.

ROSEBUD

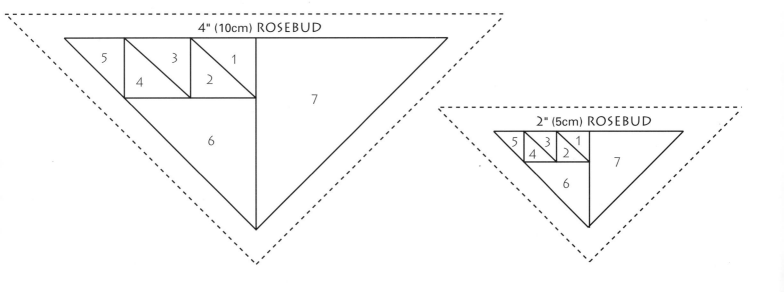

4" (10cm) ROSEBUD

2" (5cm) ROSEBUD

Creative options

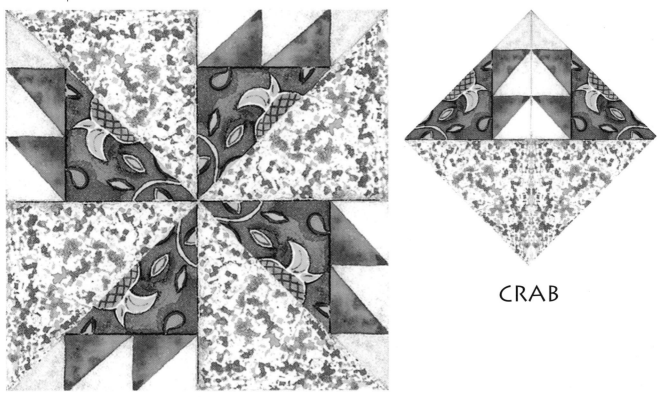

CRAB

PALM FROND

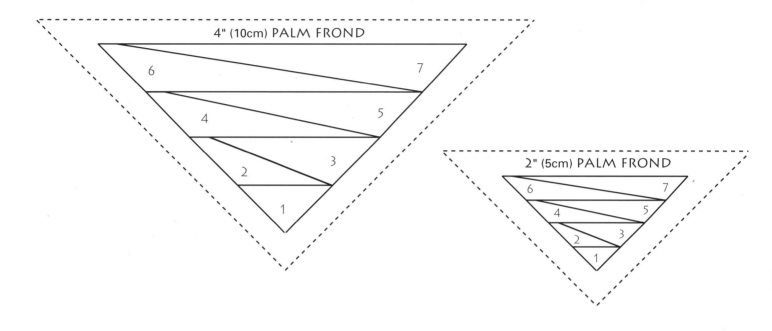

4" (10cm) PALM FROND

2" (5cm) PALM FROND

Creative options

CROSS AND CROWN

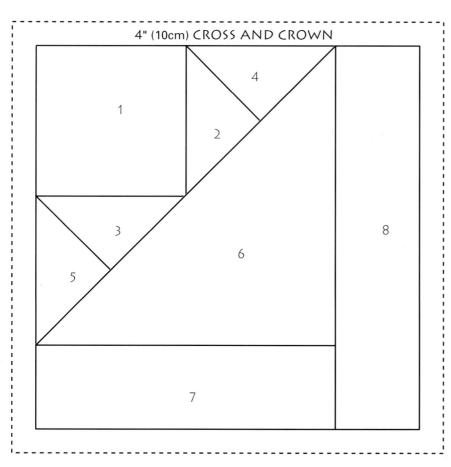

4" (10cm) CROSS AND CROWN

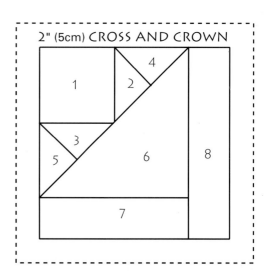

2" (5cm) CROSS AND CROWN

Creative options

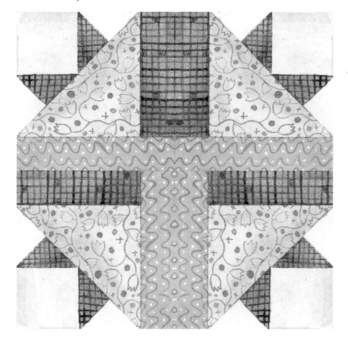

PINEBURR BEAUTY

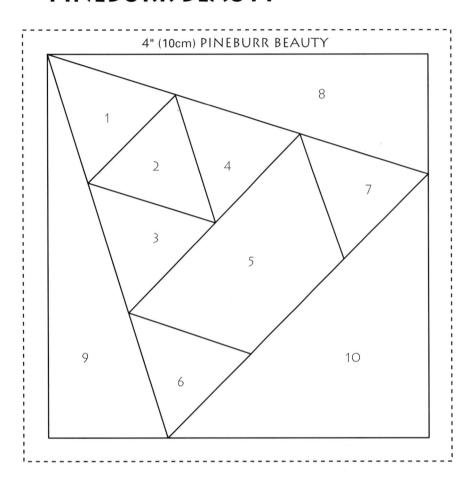

4" (10cm) PINEBURR BEAUTY

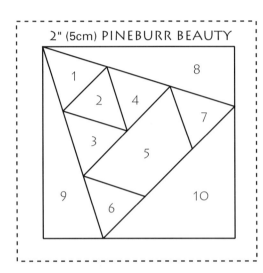

2" (5cm) PINEBURR BEAUTY

Creative option

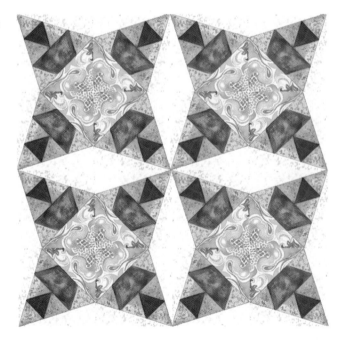

CROCUS

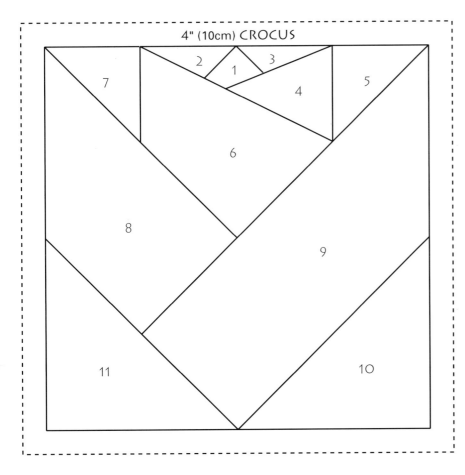

4" (10cm) CROCUS

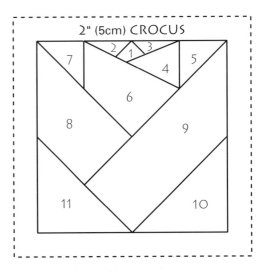

2" (5cm) CROCUS

Creative options

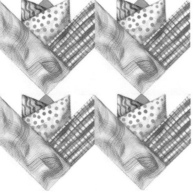

DELECTABLE MOUNTAINS

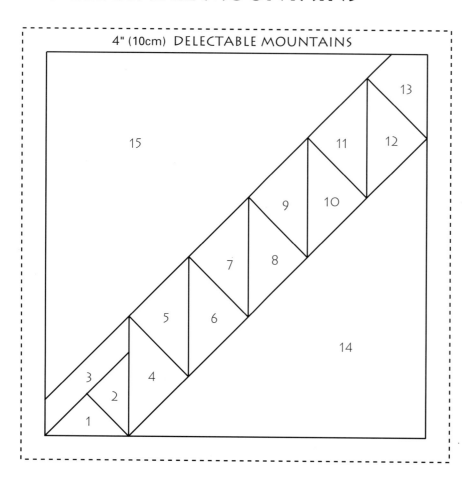

4" (10cm) DELECTABLE MOUNTAINS

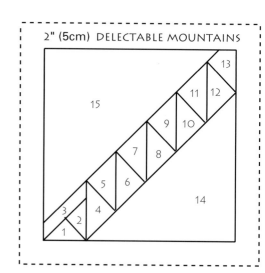

2" (5cm) DELECTABLE MOUNTAINS

Creative option

FARMHOUSE BEST

Pull out your scraps and tidbits and enjoy a playful experiment with color, pattern, and texture while making these designs. The result may be a "homey" quilt in the best sense.

INTERLACED STAR ♦♦

This patchwork pattern is a personal favorite. It looks complex but is easy to assemble from four subunits for a block, several for a border. Play with color choices to achieve the interlaced look.

BABY BLOCKS ♦

This pattern was a popular one in Victorian times and is still popular today. There are many possible variants. You can easily assemble the subunits into rows. Color a layout design to experiment with stars and three-dimensional effects.

NOTE: If you use older, worn fabrics, they may need some extra support. A fabric foundation will help, or fuse lightweight interfacing to their backs.

GARRET WINDOW ◆

This is a very easy traditional patchwork pattern, first published in *American Needlewoman*. It has some interesting layout variations—try these arrangements, as well as your own!

COUNTRY COUSINS ◆◆◆

This is a very basic patchwork block that will make many patterns. If you choose the right fabrics, you

can see fish motifs, but Xs, hourglasses, and broken-dish patterns are also possibilities. This makes an excellent scrap quilt.

BUTTERFLIES ◆◆

Choose bright scraps for a lively finished quilt, full of fluttering wings. You'll find the subunit assembly very easy.

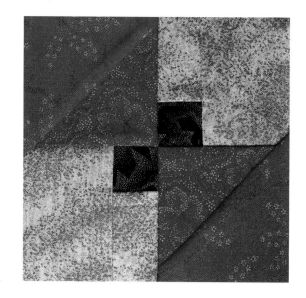

INTERLACED STAR

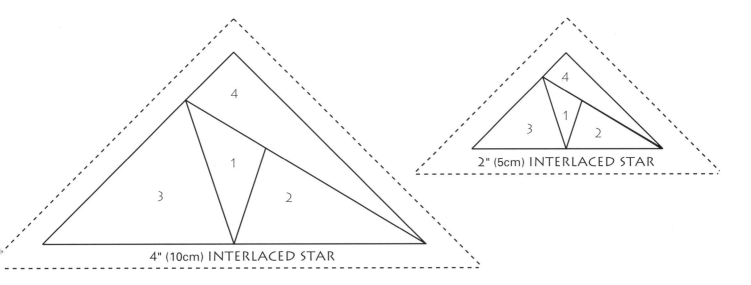

4" (10cm) INTERLACED STAR

2" (5cm) INTERLACED STAR

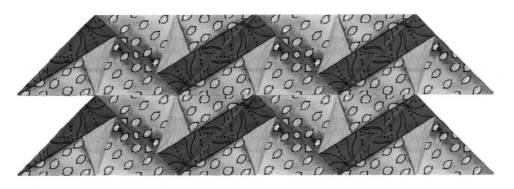

Creative options

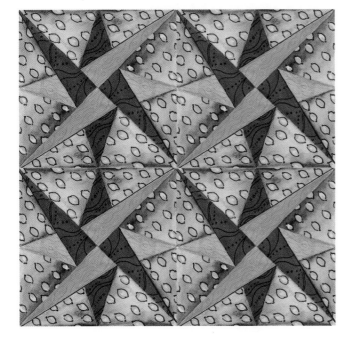

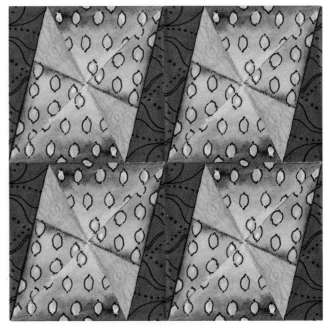

BABY BLOCKS

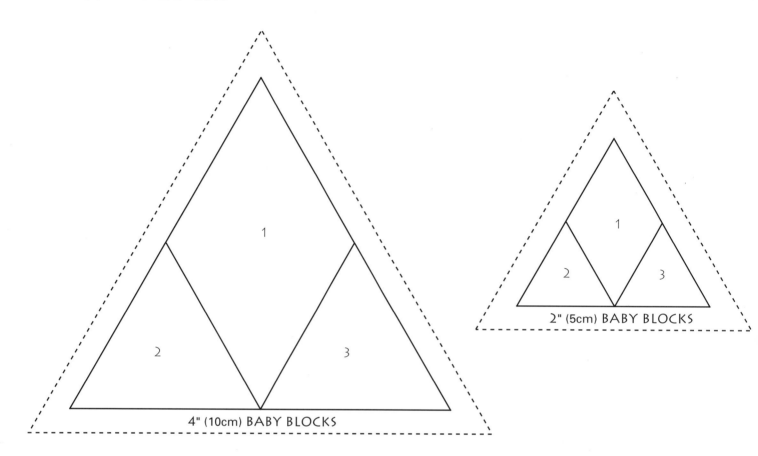

4" (10cm) BABY BLOCKS

2" (5cm) BABY BLOCKS

Creative options

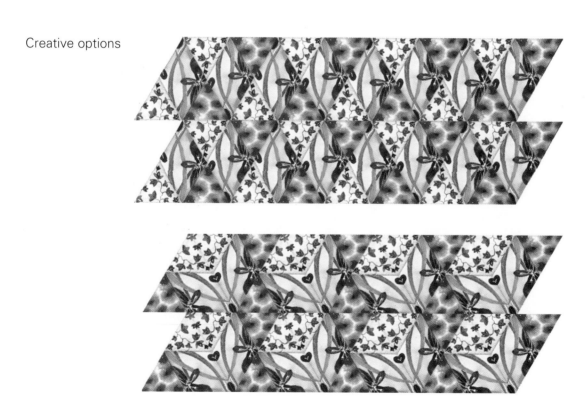

BABY BLOCK COLORING/DESIGN SHEET

GARRET WINDOW

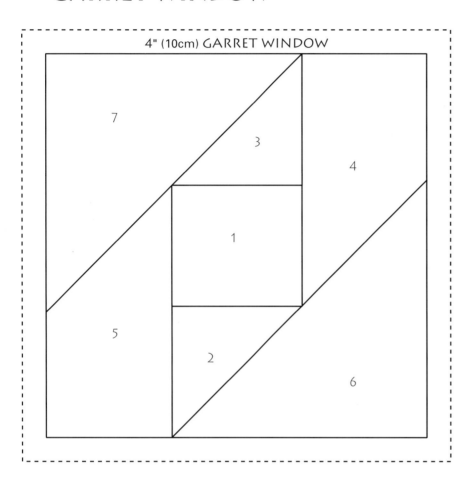

4" (10cm) GARRET WINDOW

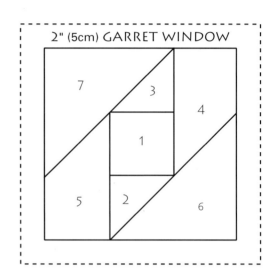

2" (5cm) GARRET WINDOW

Creative options

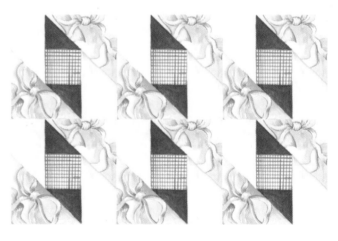

COUNTRY COUSINS

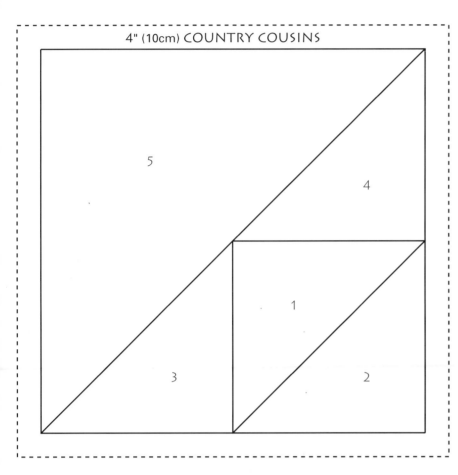

4" (10cm) COUNTRY COUSINS

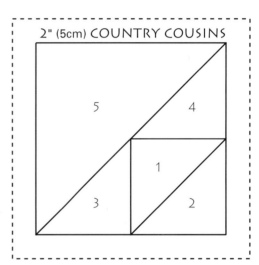

2" (5cm) COUNTRY COUSINS

Creative option

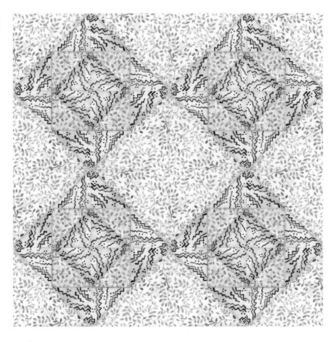

BUTTERFLIES

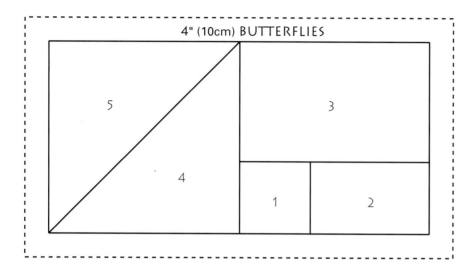

4" (10cm) BUTTERFLIES

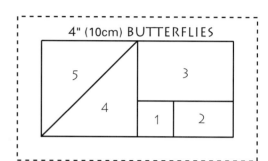

4" (10cm) BUTTERFLIES

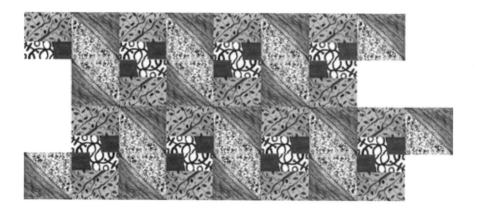

Creative options

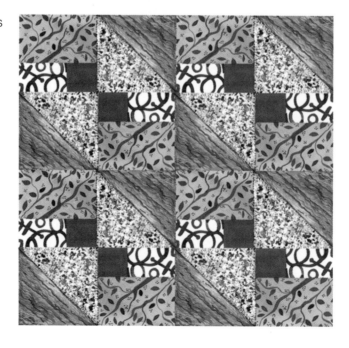

ROYAL VICTORIAN

Victorian needlewomen enjoyed displaying their skills with striking counterpoint designs. These patterns are sure to produce brilliant graphic quilts, eye-catching and impressive, to exhibit modern needle skills as well.

ANNA'S CHOICE ◆◆

A very simple block with an easy subunit assembly, this pattern is nevertheless striking in its positive/negative effects. Imagine one subunit alone for a kite design!

VARIABLE STAR ◆◆◆

This is a counterpoint version of the beloved Sawtooth Star or Ohio Star pattern. If the central star is colored from all the same fabrics, you will

get a lovely Evening Star result. Despite the "variables" of piecing the two subunits, this one is worth the work.

NIGHT AND DAY ◆◆◆

A beautiful counterpoint pattern. Careful fabric selection will make the stars appear three-dimensional and elegantly faceted, like a real gem.

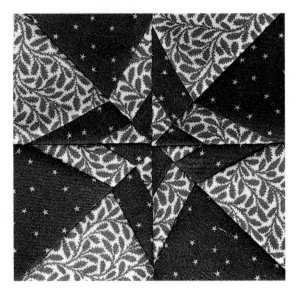

GRETCHEN ◆◆◆

Actually a simpler subunit assembly than some counterpoint patterns, this block offers some exciting diagonal movement when used in an overall block layout format.

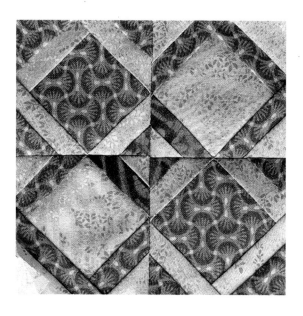

DOUBLE PINWHEEL ◆◆◆

This pattern of two subunits will yield striking overall effects when colored in counterpoint style. It's well worth the work of matching seams.

HOURGLASS ◆◆

This is an easy block to use for counterpoint coloring. The "hourglass" figures that result from matching the corners also look like the windings on spools of thread. Choose your fabrics to make the desired motifs stand out. This is traditionally made in red and white.

ANNA'S CHOICE

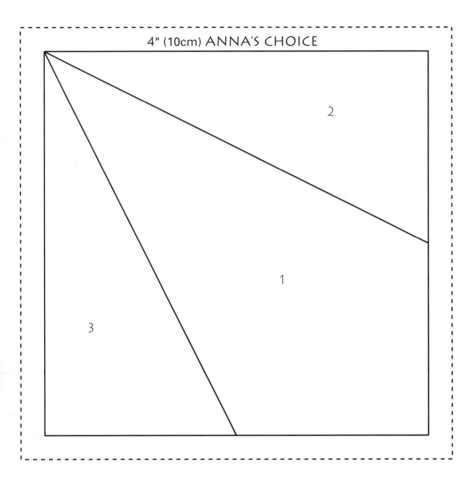

4" (10cm) ANNA'S CHOICE

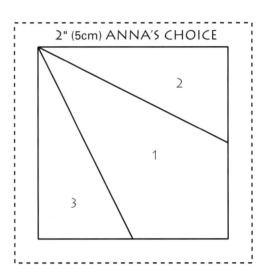

2" (5cm) ANNA'S CHOICE

Creative option

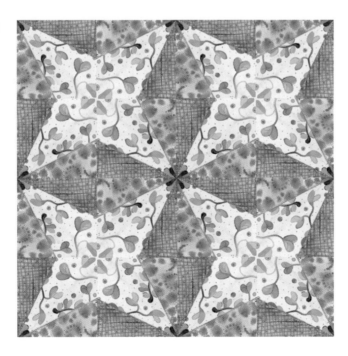

VARIABLE STAR

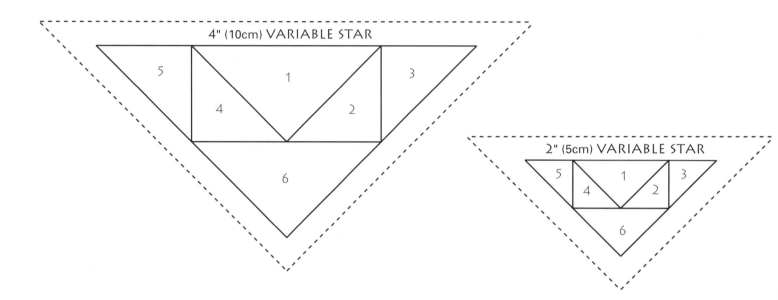

4" (10cm) VARIABLE STAR

2" (5cm) VARIABLE STAR

Creative option

NIGHT AND DAY

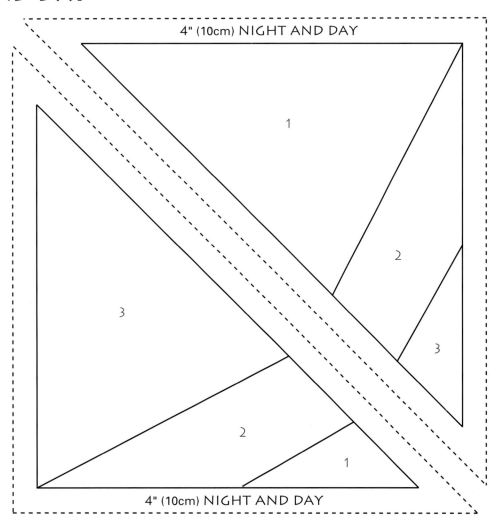

4" (10cm) NIGHT AND DAY

1

2

3

3

2

1

4" (10cm) NIGHT AND DAY

Creative option

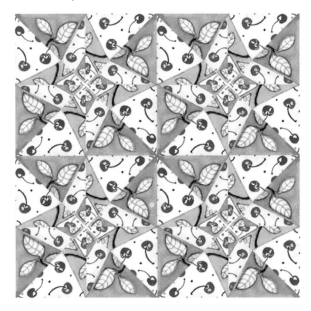

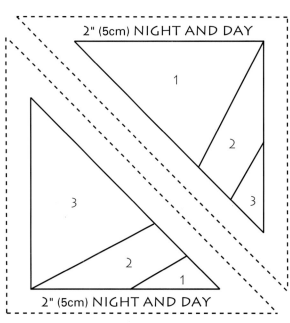

2" (5cm) NIGHT AND DAY

1

2

3

3

2

1

2" (5cm) NIGHT AND DAY

GRETCHEN

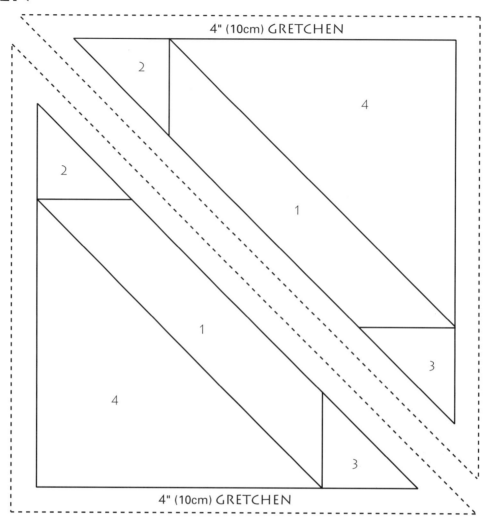

4" (10cm) GRETCHEN

2

2

4

1

1

4

3

3

4" (10cm) GRETCHEN

Creative option

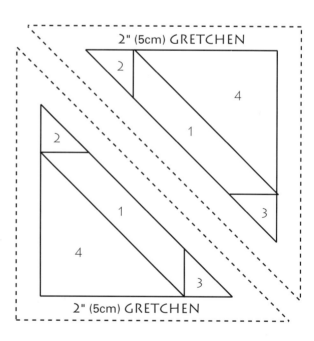

2" (5cm) GRETCHEN

2

2

4

1

1

3

4

3

2" (5cm) GRETCHEN

HOURGLASS

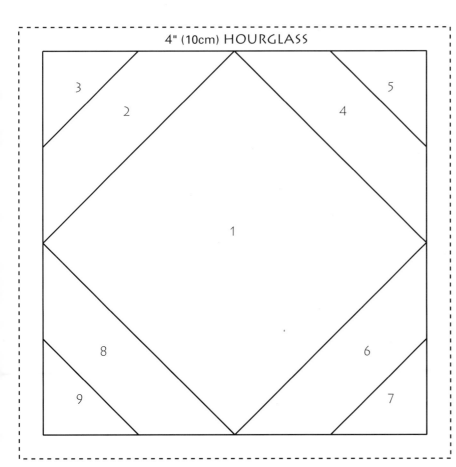

4" (10cm) HOURGLASS

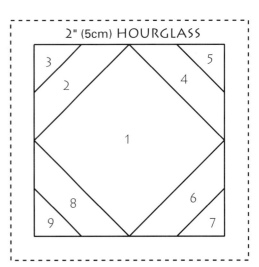

2" (5cm) HOURGLASS

Creative option

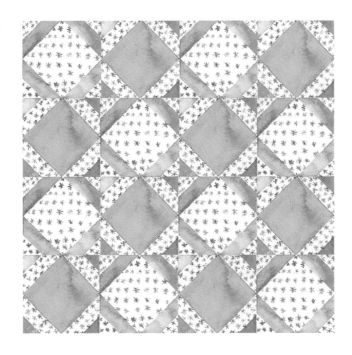

DOUBLE PINWHEEL

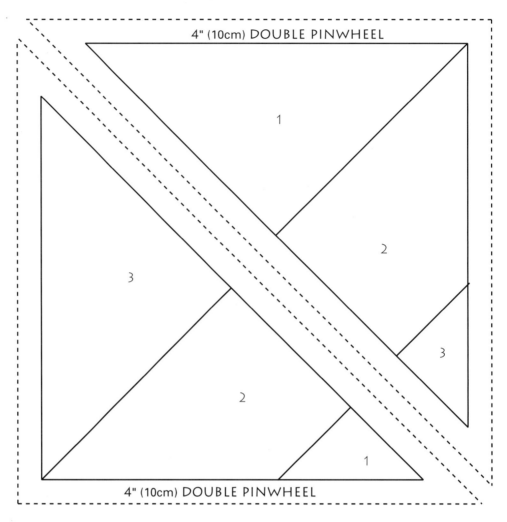

4" (10cm) DOUBLE PINWHEEL

4" (10cm) DOUBLE PINWHEEL

Creative option

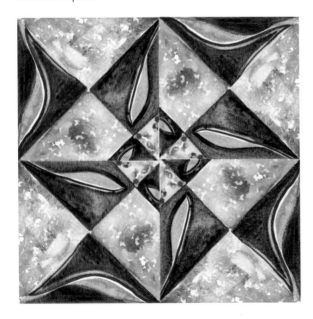

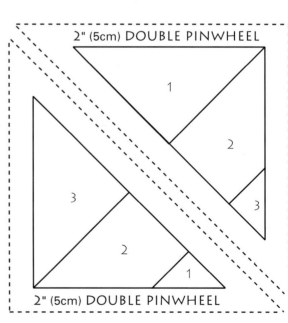

2" (5cm) DOUBLE PINWHEEL

2" (5cm) DOUBLE PINWHEEL

PATRIOTIC FEVER

Red, white, and blue has always been a favorite color scheme in American history. Quilters today, as in the past centuries, can express their political and patriotic sentiments in fabric with these designs.

BALLOT BOX ◆

When American women stitched this block, they had patriotic fever, but not the vote. Make this block and celebrate the triumphs of our suffragette foremothers.

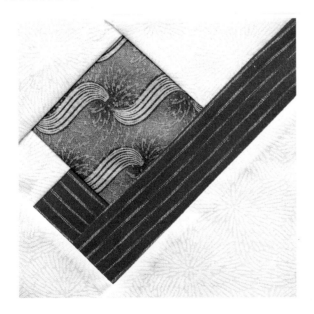

KING'S CROSS ◆◆

Choose striking fabrics for this favorite traditional block to bring out the overall design. Experiment with block layouts—there are some interesting variations.

ROMAN CANDLE ◆◆

This is an easy pattern for making at least two types of stars. What patriotic celebration would be complete without fireworks to brighten the sky?

VICTORY ◆◆

A more complicated version of Roman Candle, this pattern has an exciting sense of movement. Experiment with layouts, as you can make many different stars.

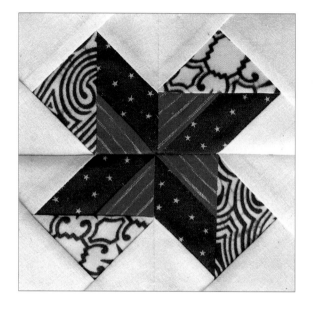

MARINER'S STAR ◆ TO ◆◆◆

Made singly, this pattern yields a crisp, graphic sailboat. Joined together into a star as shown, it can yield exciting dimensional results.

OLD GLORY ◆

No patriotic quilt would be complete without the flag. Traditional color choices will yield the beloved favorite; more contemporary fabrics can infuse sharp "arty" flavor to your quilt.

FLYING PINWHEEL ◆◆

Use bright colors to make this pinwheel star spin inside its framing border triangles. This makes an excellent scrap quilt.

BALLOT BOX

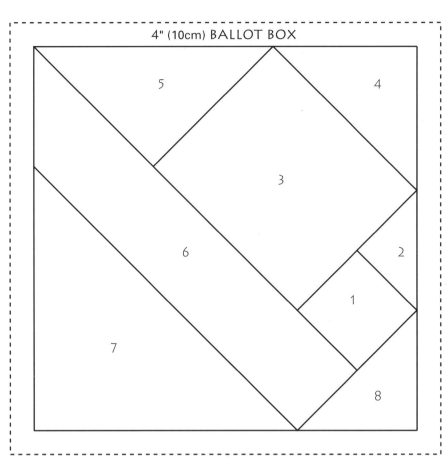

4" (10cm) BALLOT BOX

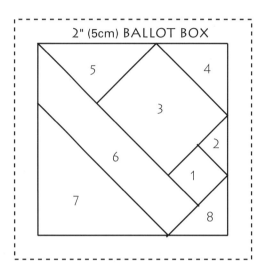

2" (5cm) BALLOT BOX

Creative option

KING'S CROSS

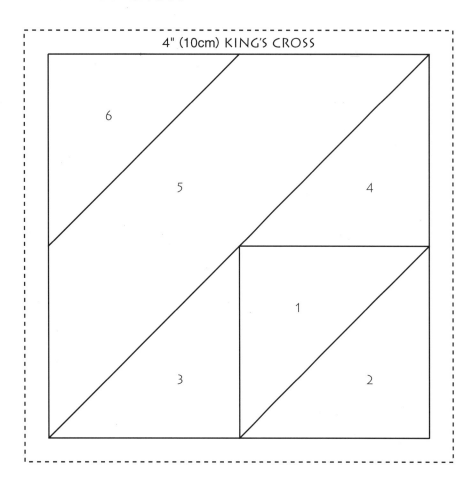

4" (10cm) KING'S CROSS

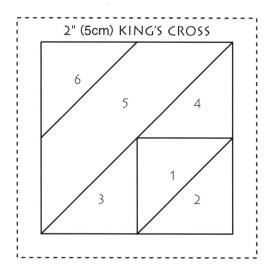

2" (5cm) KING'S CROSS

Creative option

ROMAN CANDLE

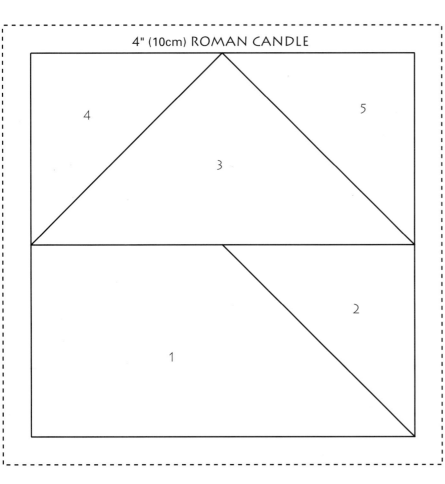

4" (10cm) ROMAN CANDLE

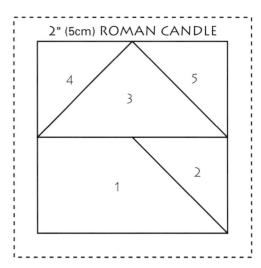

2" (5cm) ROMAN CANDLE

Creative options

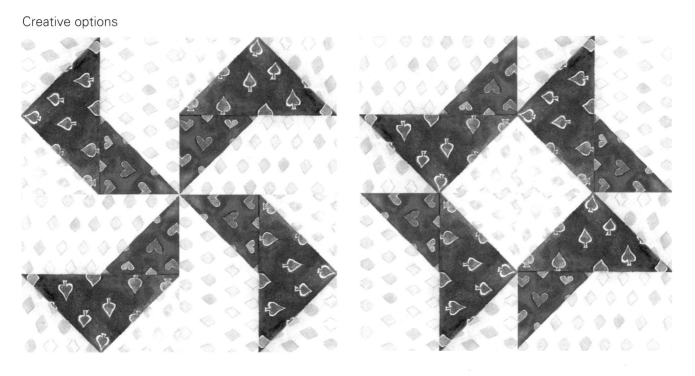

VICTORY

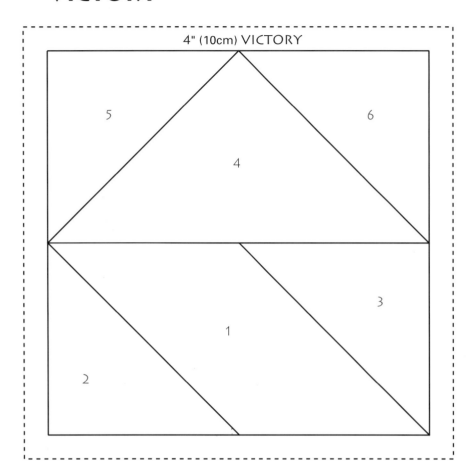

4" (10cm) VICTORY

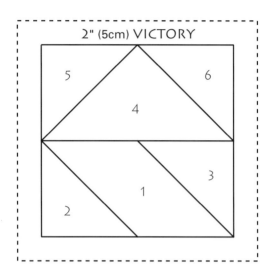

2" (5cm) VICTORY

Creative option

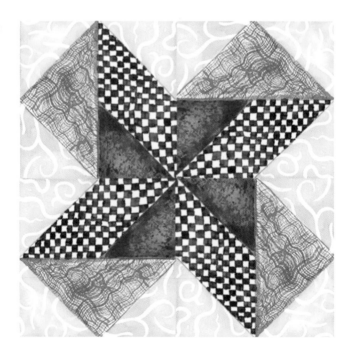

FLYING PINWHEEL

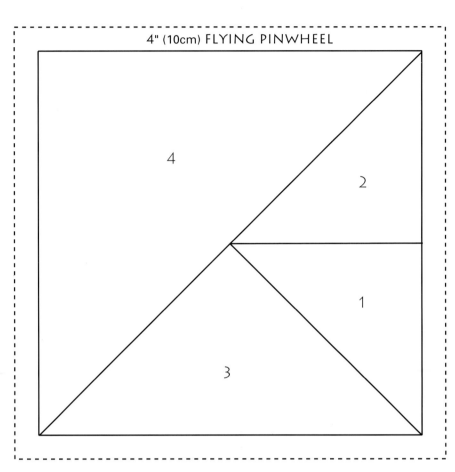

4" (10cm) FLYING PINWHEEL

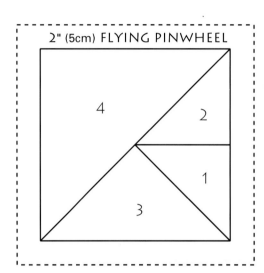

2" (5cm) FLYING PINWHEEL

Creative option

MARINER'S STAR

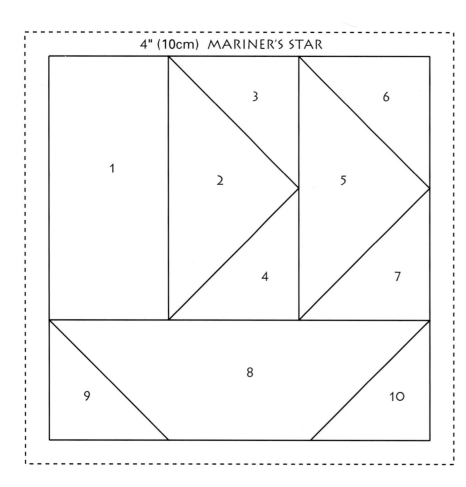

4" (10cm) MARINER'S STAR

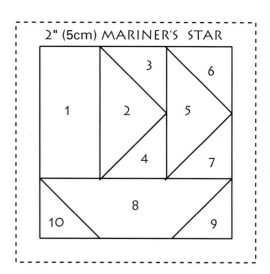

2" (5cm) MARINER'S STAR

Creative option

OLD GLORY

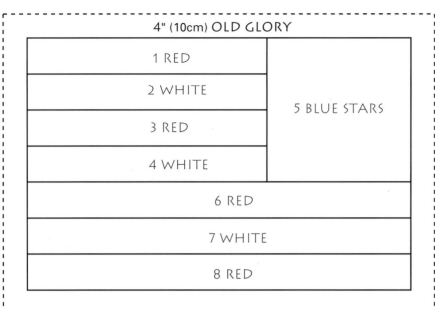

4" (10cm) OLD GLORY

1 RED	
2 WHITE	
3 RED	5 BLUE STARS
4 WHITE	
6 RED	
7 WHITE	
8 RED	

2" (5cm) OLD GLORY

1 RED	
2 WHITE	5 BLUE STARS
3 RED	
4 WHITE	
6 RED	
7 WHITE	
8 RED	

Creative option

WESTWARD HO!

The Victorian era continued the great westward expansion in America and the settlement of Australia, Canada, and New Zealand in the Crown Colonies. Many were the partings of loved ones and the hardships of the pioneer life; it is fitting that needleworkers chose patchwork blocks that commemorated their journey. Select one of these patterns to recapture that pioneer vigor in your quilts.

WHICH WAY SOUTH ◆◆

This block is a variant of the popular Flying Geese motif. Consider it to make a pretty scrap quilt.

OH SUSANNAH ◆

This simple block was first published by the Ladies Art Circle around 1900. It makes a wonderful variety of different patterns, depending on the block orientation in the assembly layout. The traditional name recalls the song of that era, still popular today.

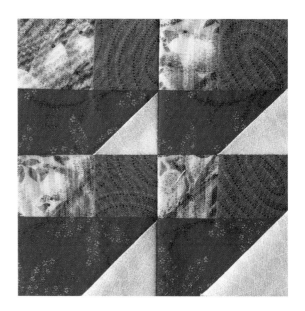

THUNDERBIRD ◆

This block pays homage to the various Native American peoples who were displaced by the westward pioneer movements. Use the layouts shown, or play with the blocks to create your own design.

INDIAN TRAIL ◆◆

This easy traditional block with its strong geometrics can result in very graphic art quilts. It can be an effective scrap quilt as well.

TALL PINE TREE ◆

Was the designer of this pattern thinking longingly of the woods back home as she sewed in her new prairie surroundings, or celebrating the stupendous firs of the Pacific Northwest? This pattern offers the modern quilter ample opportunity for scrap play and graphic results.

TURKEY TRACKS ◆

A prickly variation of the original block, this pattern gives plenty of opportunity for color and layout play.

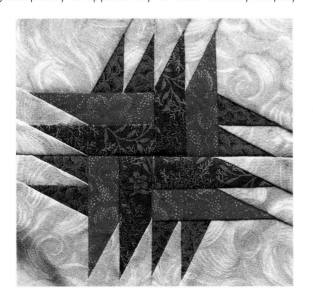

ROCKY ROAD TO KANSAS ◆◆

This pattern is as old as wagon trains and pioneer brides. Enjoy the string piecing and use up your tiny, much-loved and hoarded scraps.

WHICH WAY SOUTH

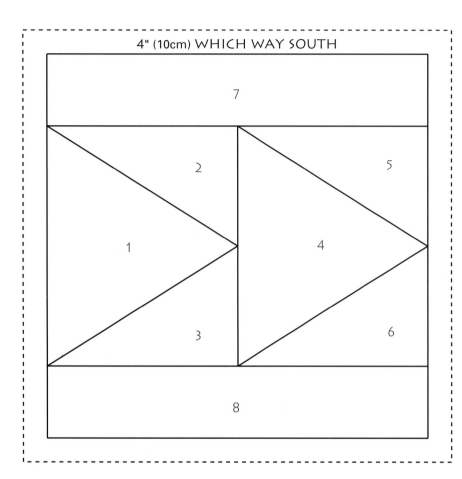

4" (10cm) WHICH WAY SOUTH

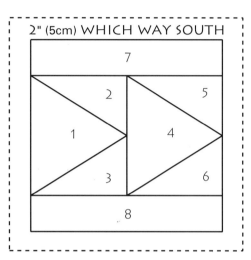

2" (5cm) WHICH WAY SOUTH

Creative option

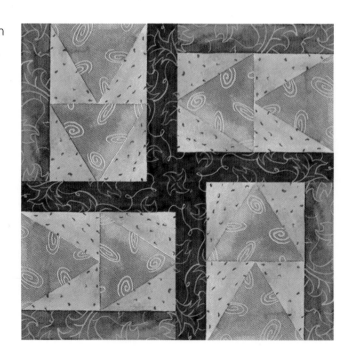

OH SUSANNAH

4" (10cm) OH SUSANNAH

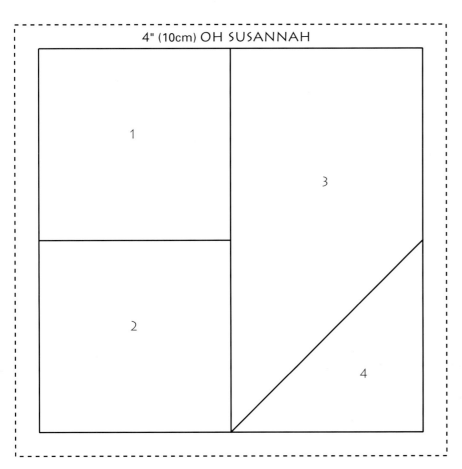

2" (5cm) OH SUSANNAH

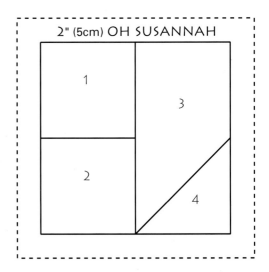

Creative options

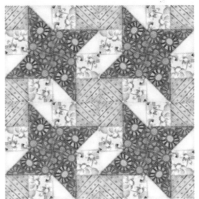

THUNDERBIRD

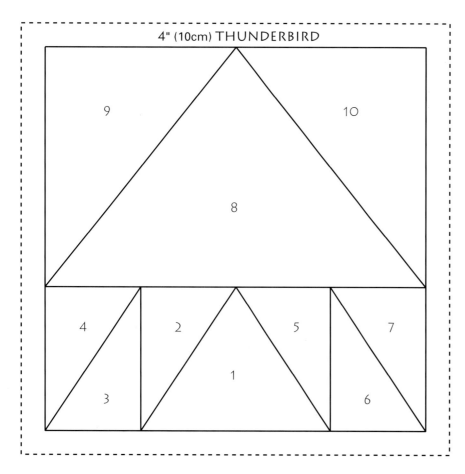

4" (10cm) THUNDERBIRD

9   10

8

4   2   5   7

1

3   6

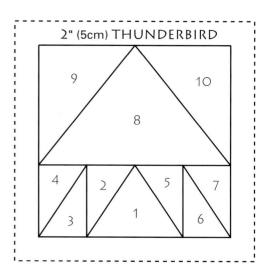

2" (5cm) THUNDERBIRD

9   10

8

4   2   5   7

3   1   6

Creative options

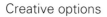

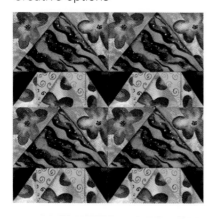

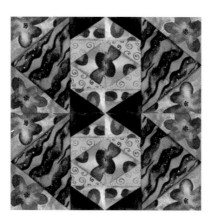

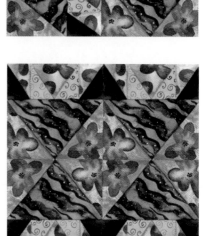

INDIAN TRAIL

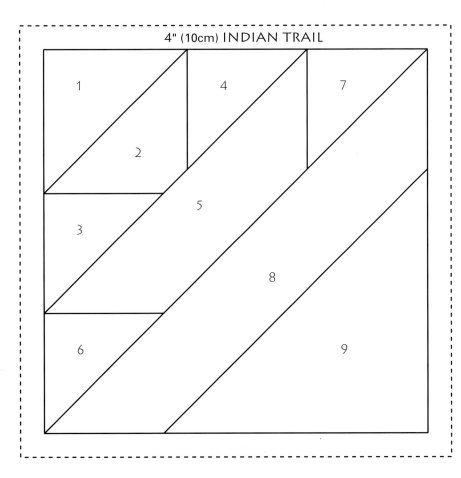

4" (10cm) INDIAN TRAIL

1   4   7

2

5

3

8

6   9

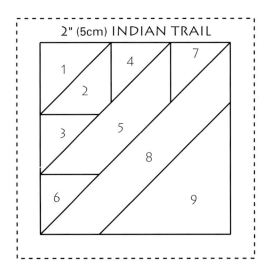

2" (5cm) INDIAN TRAIL

1   4   7

2

3   5

8

6   9

Creative options

TURKEY TRACKS

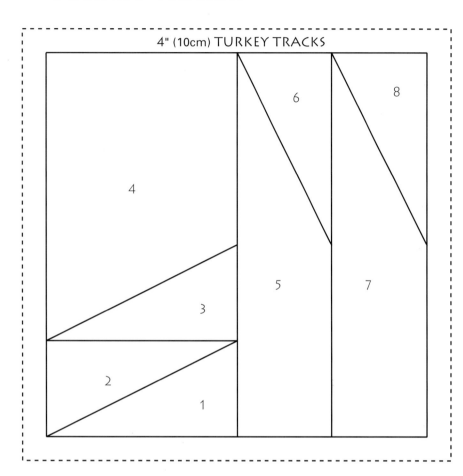

4" (10cm) TURKEY TRACKS

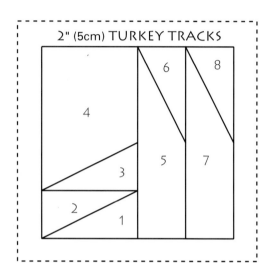

2" (5cm) TURKEY TRACKS

Creative options

TALL PINE TREE

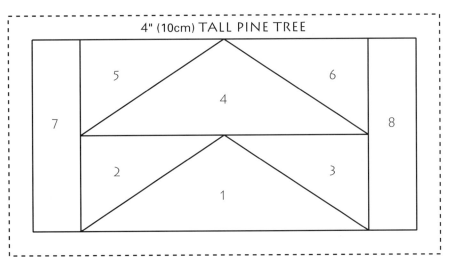

4" (10cm) TALL PINE TREE

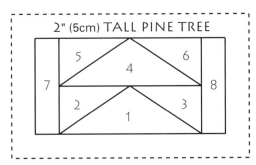

2" (5cm) TALL PINE TREE

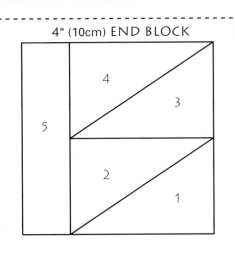

4" (10cm) END BLOCK

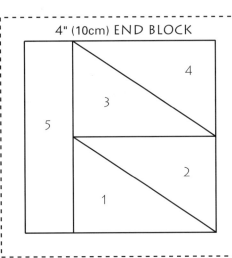

4" (10cm) END BLOCK

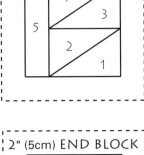

2" (5cm) END BLOCK

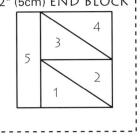

2" (5cm) END BLOCK

Creative option

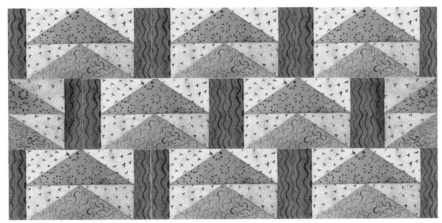

ROCKY ROAD TO KANSAS

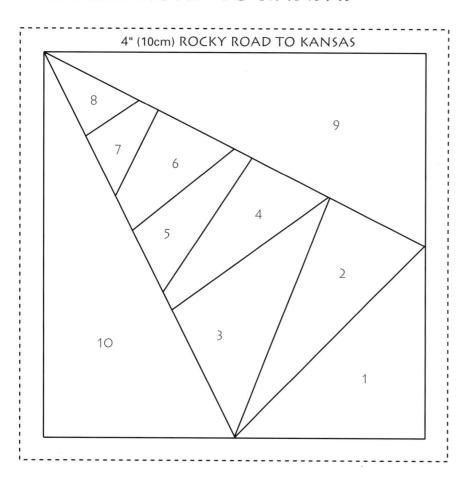

4" (10cm) ROCKY ROAD TO KANSAS

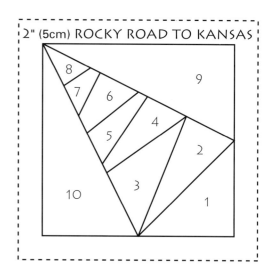

2" (5cm) ROCKY ROAD TO KANSAS

Creative option

FOND MEMORIES

With people moving more frequently due to westward expansion and the Industrial Revolution, separations and partings became more common to Americans. Friendship blocks and quilt exchanges were ways to cling to loved ones far away. Today's quilters may also wish to create personalized commemorative gifts. Signatures should be in permanent ink, or heat-set for permanence. Use the paper foundation to trace a centered name, sentiment, or drawn motif.

FRIENDSHIP CHARM ◆

Based on a very simple traditional pattern, this makes an excellent friendship exchange block. Get together with a group of your quilting friends and exchange either fabric scraps or signed blocks.

FOND MEMORY ◆ TO ◆◆◆

This block is based on a modified sailboat motif and yields a nice framing square for signatures or a rotating star for sets of names. Choose background colors carefully for signature clarity.

PICTURE FRAME ◆

Refer to Jean Ray Laury's book, *Imagery on Fabric*, for a variety of methods available for color or "antique" style photo prints on fabric. Alternatively, you can frame a favorite fabric motif or rubber-stamp image.

DIAMOND MEMORIES ♦♦

A more complex framing pattern, this block in a 4" (10cm) version (or larger) still gives ample space for featuring favorite photos or images on your quilt.

FRIENDSHIP AUTOGRAPH ♦

This is a very simple but popular traditional autograph pattern. Make several to exchange with your quilting friends or make blanks to be signed by family members at the next reunion or celebration.

ALBUM ♦

A beloved Victorian era pattern, this block design offers room for autographs or photo memories. An excellent scrap quilt opportunity as well.

REMEMBRANCE ♦

A beautiful scrap friendship pattern, this block was taken from a quilt made for Betsy Wright Lee in the late 1800s. (You can read about Betsy's life and see her quilt in Linda Otto Lipsett's book, *Remember Me*.) This, too, makes an excellent block to exchange.

FOND MEMORY

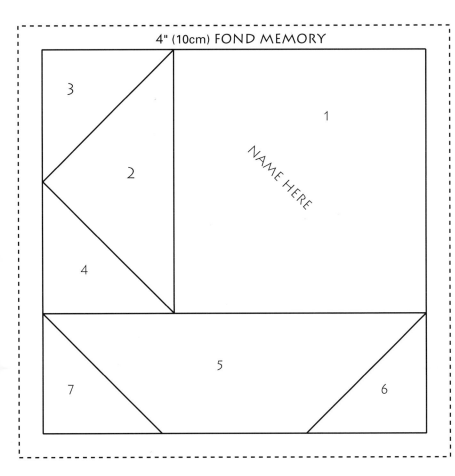

4" (10cm) FOND MEMORY

3

1

2

NAME HERE

4

5

7

6

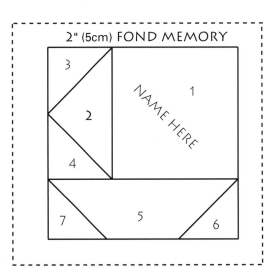

2" (5cm) FOND MEMORY

3

1

2

NAME HERE

4

7

5

6

Creative options

FRIENDSHIP CHARM

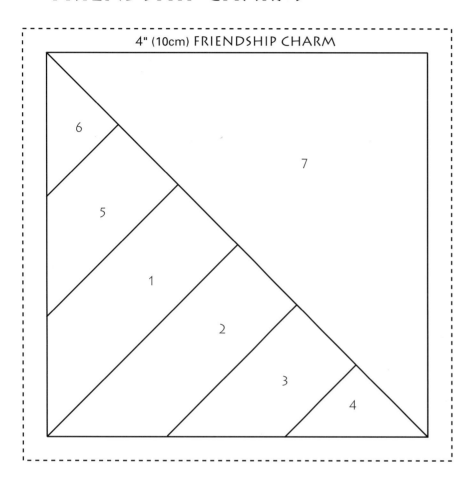

4" (10cm) FRIENDSHIP CHARM

6
5
7
1
2
3
4

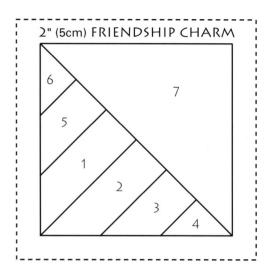

2" (5cm) FRIENDSHIP CHARM

6
5
7
1
2
3
4

Creative options

PICTURE FRAME

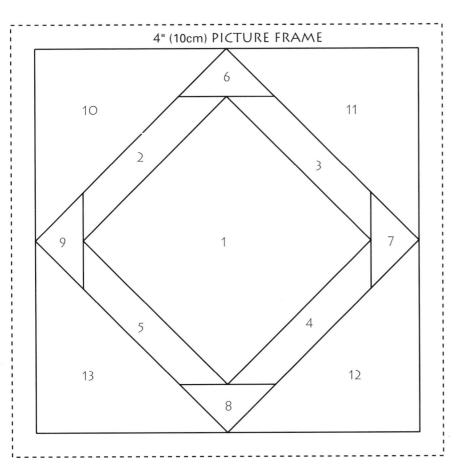

4" (10cm) PICTURE FRAME

10   6   11
2   3
9   1   7
5   4
13   8   12

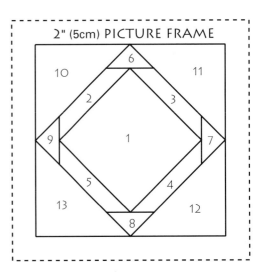

2" (5cm) PICTURE FRAME

10   6   11
2   3
9   1   7
5   4
13   8   12

Creative option

DIAMOND MEMORIES

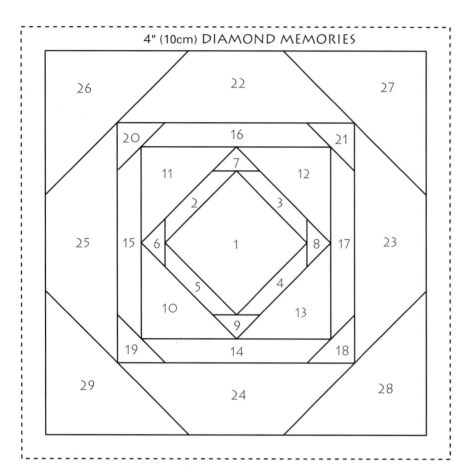

4" (10cm) DIAMOND MEMORIES

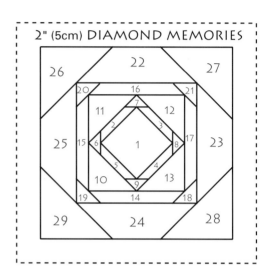

2" (5cm) DIAMOND MEMORIES

Creative option

FRIENDSHIP AUTOGRAPH

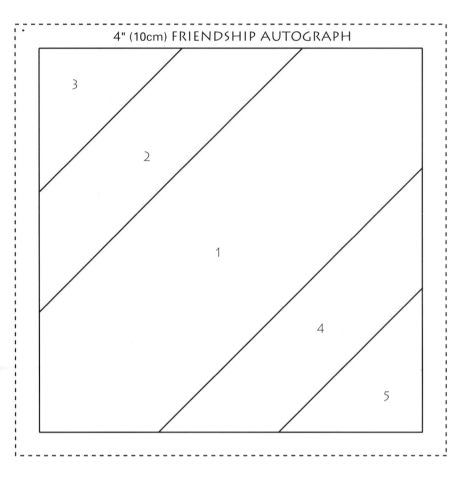

4" (10cm) FRIENDSHIP AUTOGRAPH

3

2

1

4

5

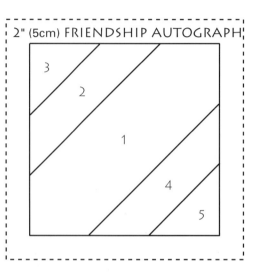

2" (5cm) FRIENDSHIP AUTOGRAPH

3

2

1

4

5

Creative options

ALBUM

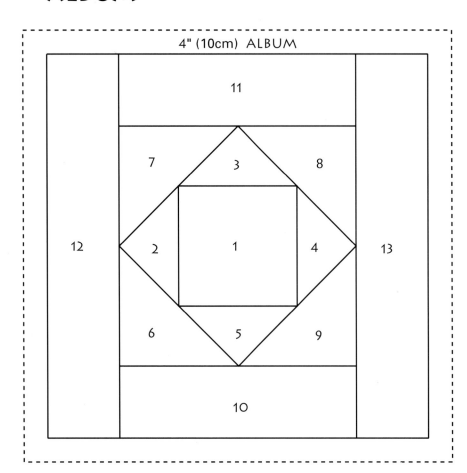

4" (10cm) ALBUM

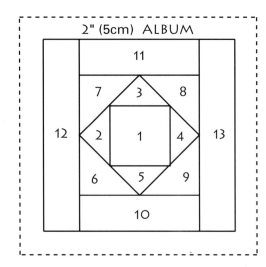

2" (5cm) ALBUM

Creative option

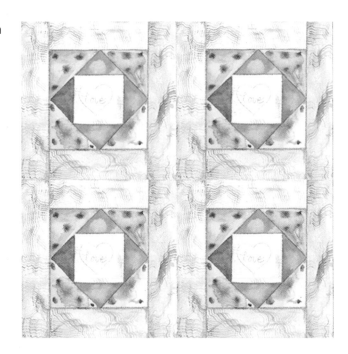

REMEMBRANCE

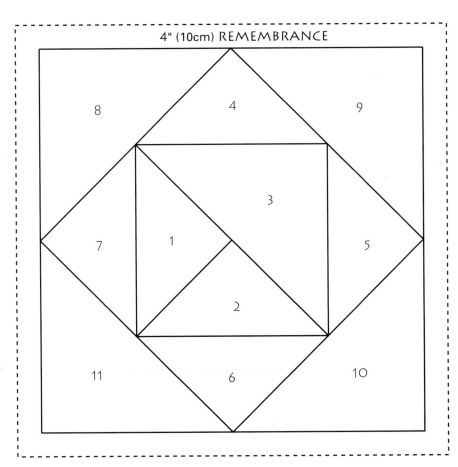

4" (10cm) REMEMBRANCE

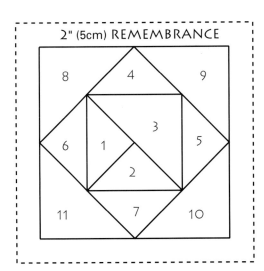

2" (5cm) REMEMBRANCE

Creative option

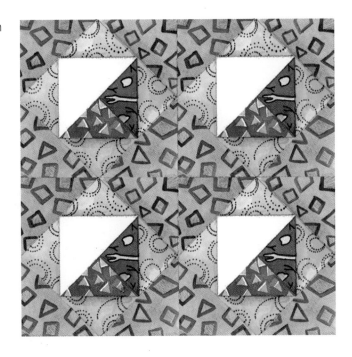

CABINS AND SILKS

The log cabin pattern has been a traditional favorite for more than a hundred years. Victorian women made many variations of this pattern, some in beautifully colored silks and satins using the new bright (almost garish to modern tastes) aniline dyed fabrics. Here are several versions of that theme.

TUMBLING SQUARES ◆

This slightly asymmetrical pattern could be used just as well for another photo-framing design. It is effective in either scrap or coordinated color layouts.

VANISHING WELL ◆

This is a rather straightforward block, though asymmetrical. It combines the classic log cabin and pineapple techniques. Careful color choice will yield a tunnel effect. Experiment with quilt layout designs: there are many exciting possibilities for an overall pattern.

CABIN GEESE ◆

This variant of pineapple log cabin was taken from an antique quilt made in 1890, shown in Kiracofe's

The American Quilt. Choose a striking color for the corner triangles—the geese—to enhance diagonal movement in your quilt.

PATIENCE ◆

This is a simplified version of the log cabin design. You can use striped fabrics for the "logs" so it seems like there are more of them.

SHOWOFF PINEAPPLE ◆◆◆

Adding diagonal rows of ever-increasing triangles brings a sense of movement to this log cabin. Careful color placement will yield some exciting circular shapes. There are numerous pieces to this block, but the construction is straightforward.

SHOWOFF LOG CABIN ◆◆◆

Log cabin quilts have been popular for more than a hundred years. Traditionally, the center square (#1) is red or yellow, and logs are alternately light and dark. Many beautiful arrangements or variations arise due to the placement of light versus dark. This particular block will display your careful construction, which is made much easier by foundation piecing.

TUMBLING SQUARES

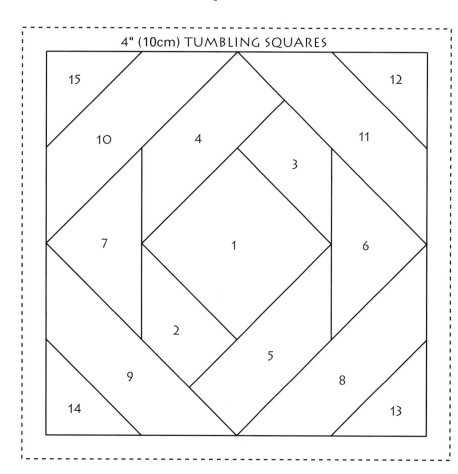

4" (10cm) TUMBLING SQUARES

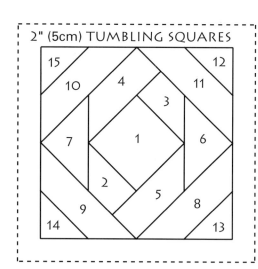

2" (5cm) TUMBLING SQUARES

Creative options

VANISHING WELL

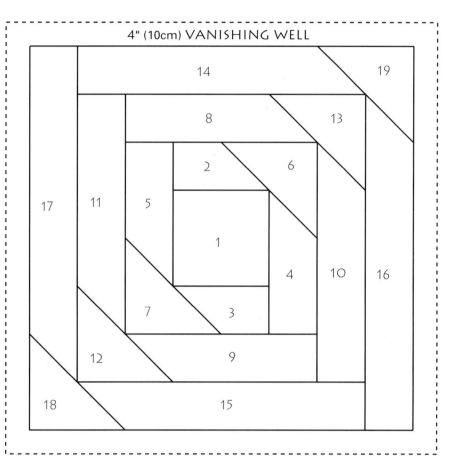

4" (10cm) VANISHING WELL

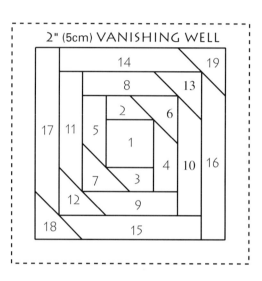

2" (5cm) VANISHING WELL

Creative options

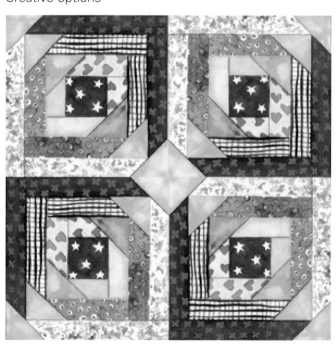

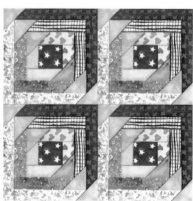

CABIN GEESE

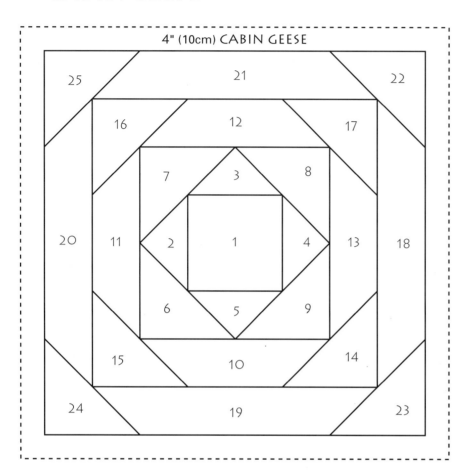

4" (10cm) CABIN GEESE

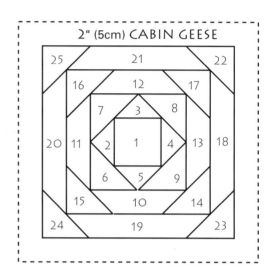

2" (5cm) CABIN GEESE

Creative option

PATIENCE

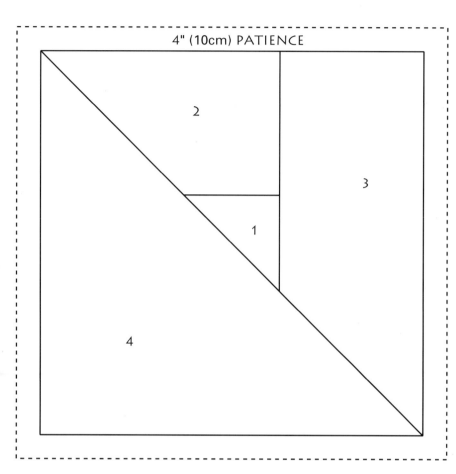

4" (10cm) PATIENCE

2

3

1

4

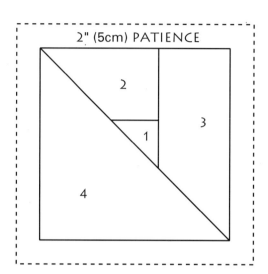

2" (5cm) PATIENCE

2

3

1

4

Creative option

SHOWOFF LOG CABIN

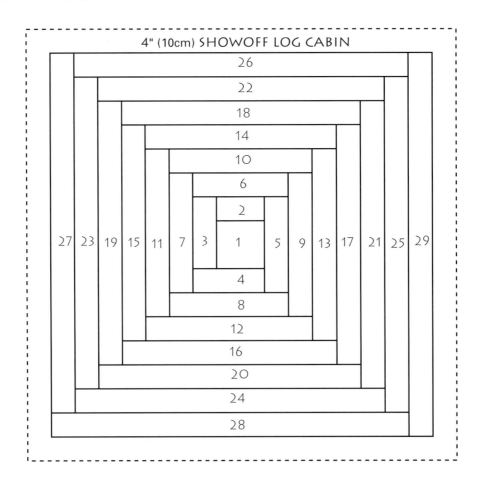

4" (10cm) SHOWOFF LOG CABIN

26
22
18
14
10
6
2
27 23 19 15 11 7 3 1 5 9 13 17 21 25 29
4
8
12
16
20
24
28

Creative option

SHOWOFF PINEAPPLE

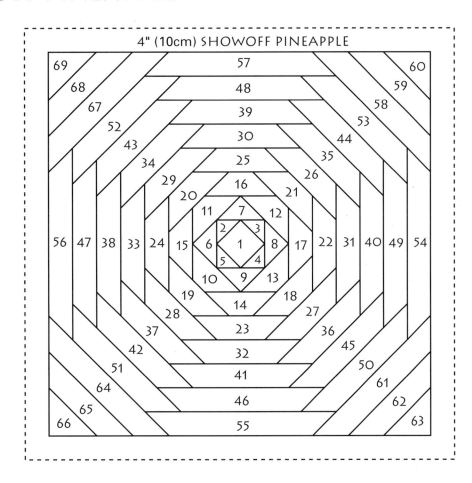

Creative option

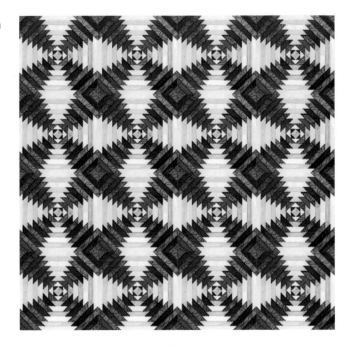

ABSTRACT/ GEOMETRIC DESIGNS

These charming blocks are sure to give any quilt a sense of excitement and movement.

FLORAL WHIRL ◆◆◆

This pattern takes patience to make but the rewards are clear. Play with color to create your own version of the hidden flowers.

FLOWER STARS ◆◆◆

These subunits make pretty diamond-shaped flowers. Assemble them into the stars shown or play with other diamond layouts.

GARDEN PATH ◆

This traditional pattern can be very effective as an outer border or in sets to make internal medallion borders. You can choose subdued fabrics for a brick walkway effect or exotic prints for an exciting frame.

GARDEN PARTY ◆

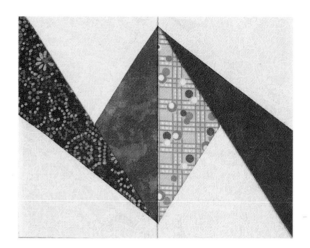

This easy geometric pattern reminds me of twinkling lights and swirling music. You can fit them into your garden individually in niches, use them for a border, or play with geometric layouts.

WHIRLING STARS ◆◆

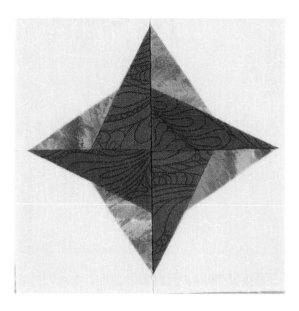

These subunits are very easy to make and to assemble into striking stars with sharp rotation. Play with pattern and fabric to create dancing energy in your quilts.

THORNY TRAIL ◆

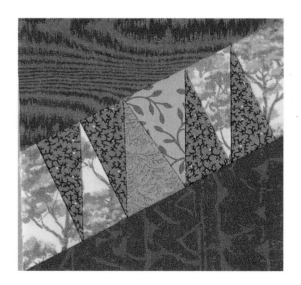

This block has great energy with its spikes and diagonal movement. You can make it in striking, high-contrast solids or an assortment of scrappy prints.

CHARMING GARDEN ◆

Select your favorite floral and leafy prints and trade charm squares with your friends. Sign your blocks with permanent markers or embroidery as a memento of friendship.

BRIGHT STARS ◆◆

One of my favorite blocks, this pattern can be dramatic or soft, bright or romantic, depending on your fabric and background choices. Worthy of a quilt to itself or as an enhancement to your garden skies.

GARDEN RAMBLE ◆◆

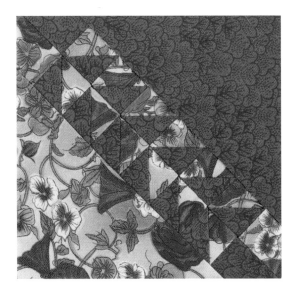

This block takes time, but is worth the effort. Enjoy choosing fabrics to make your ramble a pleasure.

FLOWER STARS

3" (7.5CM) FLOWER STARS

FLORAL WHIRL

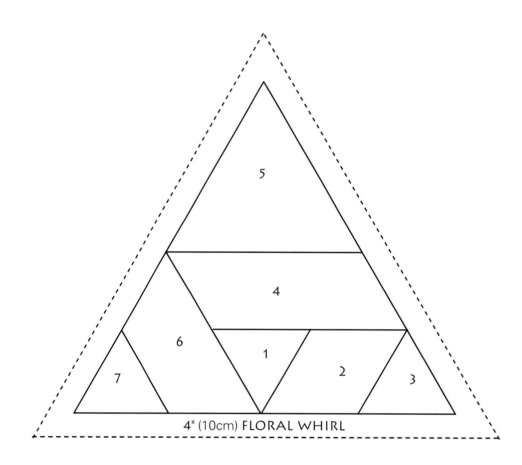

4" (10cm) FLORAL WHIRL

GARDEN PATH

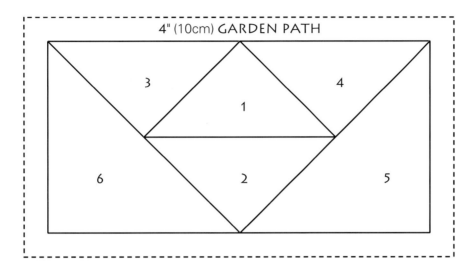

4" (10cm) GARDEN PATH

3 4 1 6 2 5

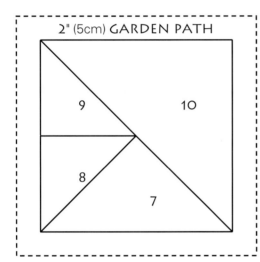

2" (5cm) GARDEN PATH

9 10 8 7

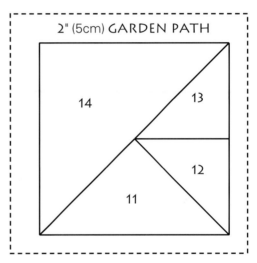

2" (5cm) GARDEN PATH

14 13 11 12

GARDEN PARTY

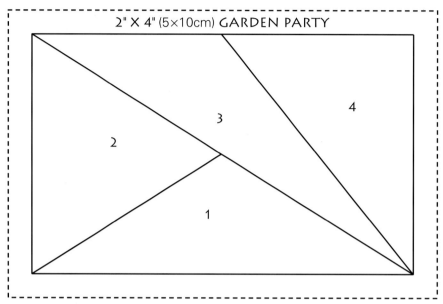

2" X 4" (5×10cm) GARDEN PARTY

2

3

4

1

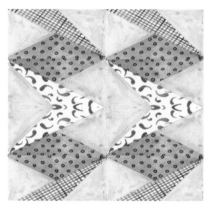

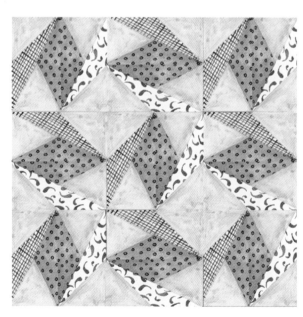

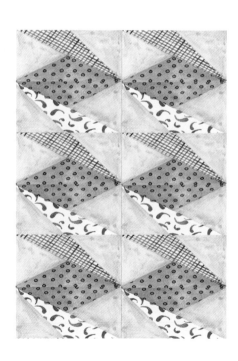

THORNY TRAIL

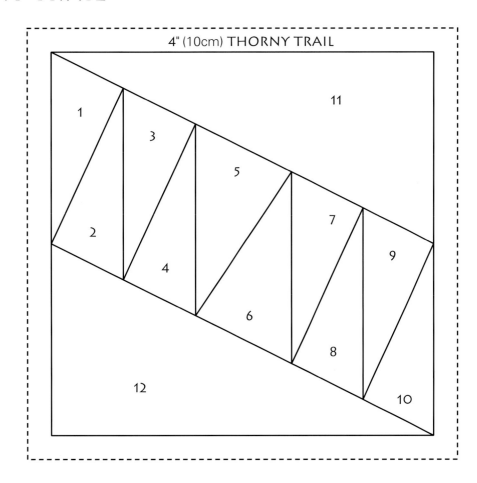

4" (10cm) THORNY TRAIL

WHIRLING STARS

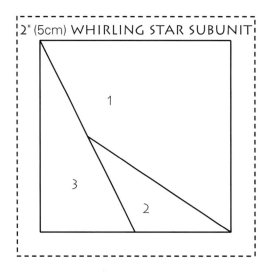

CHARMING GARDEN

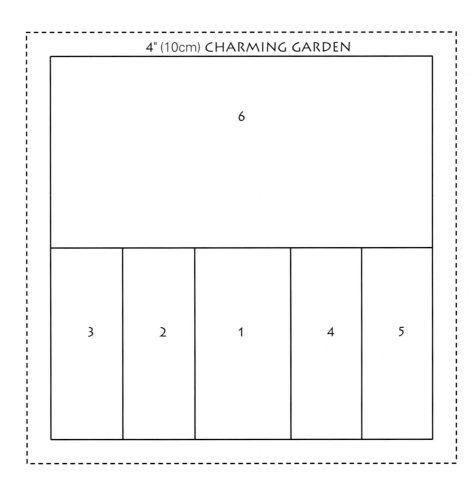

4" (10cm) CHARMING GARDEN

6

3   2   1   4   5

GARDEN RAMBLE

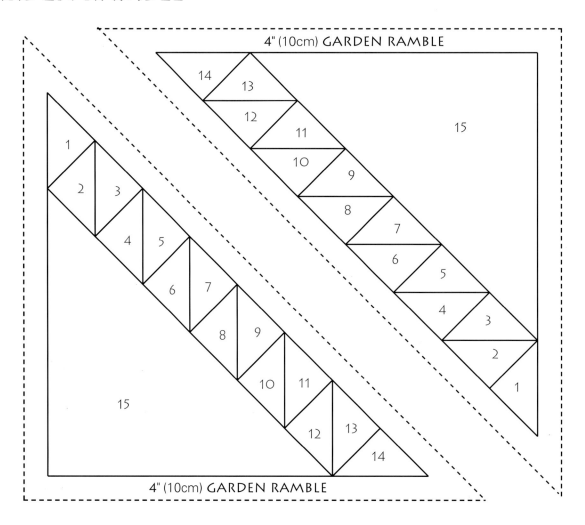

4" (10cm) GARDEN RAMBLE

14
13
12
11
10
9
8
7
6
5
4
3
2
1
15

1
2
3
4
5
6
7
8
9
10
11
12
13
14
15

4" (10cm) GARDEN RAMBLE

BRIGHT STARS

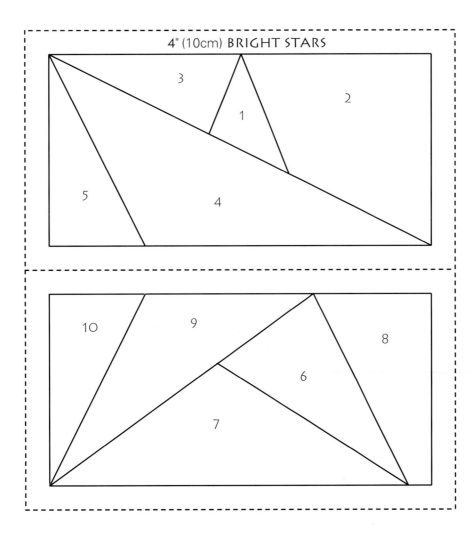

4" (10cm) BRIGHT STARS

3

1

2

5

4

10   9   8

6

7

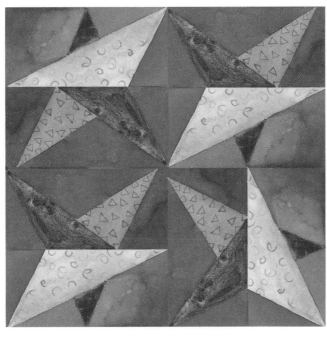

FLOWERS AND LEAVES

These delightful beauties will add a dose of springtime magic to any quilt design. Use scraps in colors as they would appear in nature, or go wild with bright, exciting colors and patterns.

CORNER BUD ◆

The subunits of this simple flower pattern are easy to make. Play with arranging them and see what nice geometrics they will form.

TALL FLOWER ◆◆◆

A short row of these striking flowers are all you need for a distinctive fabric garden. Be sure to use several shades of green fabric for more visual interest.

CLEMATIS BUD ◆

The sharp petals of this barely opening flower are a snap to create with this easy foundation pattern. Have fun arranging them into a bright quilted bouquet.

BELLFLOWER ◆

Rather fuschialike in structure, this simple flower can be made in many effective color combinations. Enjoy them in groups or singly in your fabric garden.

BIRD OF PARADISE FLOWER ◆

Dramatic and exotic, the bird of paradise is a showoff in any garden. Your fabric gardens need not be bound by reality—enjoy making these in exotic fabrics to brighten up the landscape.

AUTUMN LEAF ◆

This is a simple leaf pattern that can be made very effectively in several shades or prints. Make them in spring greens or autumn's fiery shades.

CACTUS FLOWER ◆

Full of prickly beauty, these small blocks will fit into your fabric gardens and give a natural order to your quilted landscapes.

CORNER ROSE ◆

This is a very easy pattern and makes many effective geometric arrangments for fabric gardens. Enjoy choosing the fabrics and designing your own variant.

WATER LILY ◆

Always a delightful surprise to find in the garden pond, these lilies can be made in all the colors of the rainbow at your whim.

POTTED PLANT ◆

Forcing flowering bulbs to bloom in the middle of winter while the outside greenery still sleeps is one way to salvage the sanity of a winterbound gardener. Have fun choosing special prints to make this beauty bloom especially for you.

SPIKE FLOWER ◆◆

This pattern offers a chance to play with shading and dimension in the flower garden. Its subunits are easy to put together for an effective display.

LEAF BUD ◆◆

These simple subunits yield satisfyingly sharp points on your leaves. Color them for spring, summer, or fall and enjoy their rich energy.

SPRING BUD ◆◆

Though I have named this for the first unfolding petals of spring, you can choose hot summer colors for another effect. Enjoy the ease foundation piecing gives for these sharp points.

SHARP LEAF ◆◆

This leaf offers lots of opportunity for playing with print textures and shading effects. Put some in amongst simpler foliage patterns and watch your quilt glow.

APPLE TREES ◆◆

Embellish your trees with beads or French knots to enhance their fruit tree appearance or make them in dark colors for landscape drama.

TALL FLOWER

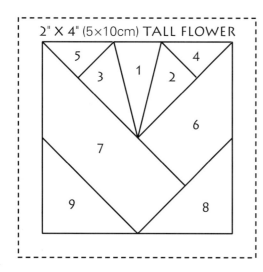

2" X 4" (5×10cm) TALL FLOWER

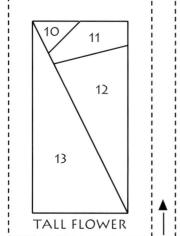

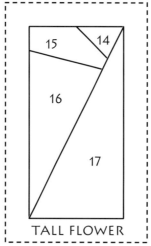

TALL FLOWER

TALL FLOWER

INSERT GREEN PIPING FOR
STEM BETWEEN SEAMS

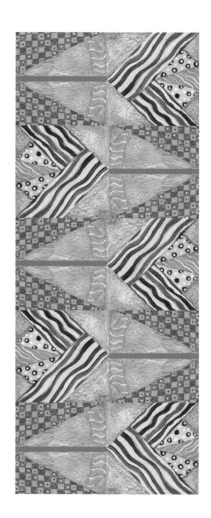

CORNER BUD

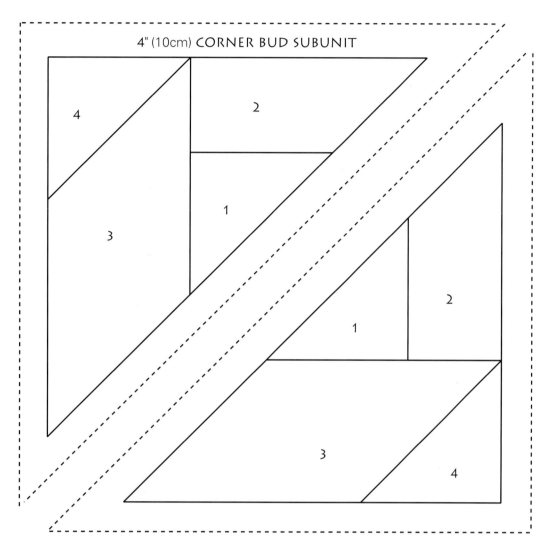

4" (10cm) CORNER BUD SUBUNIT

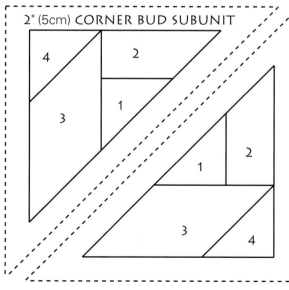

2" (5cm) CORNER BUD SUBUNIT

CLEMATIS BUD

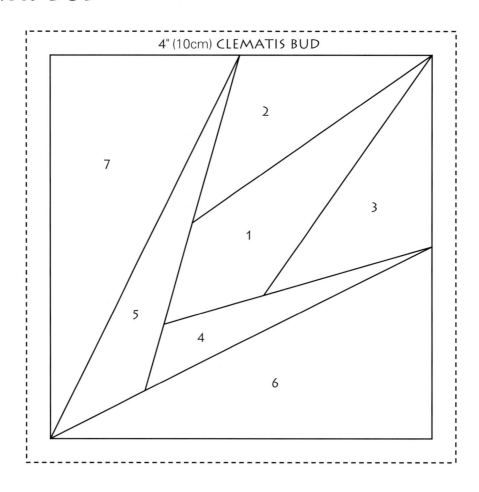

4" (10cm) CLEMATIS BUD

BELLFLOWER

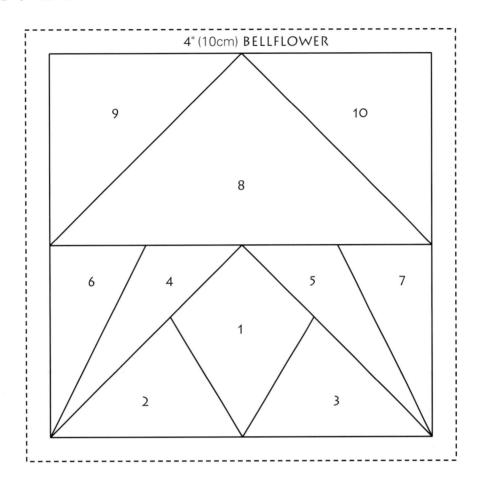

4" (10cm) BELLFLOWER

AUTUMN LEAF

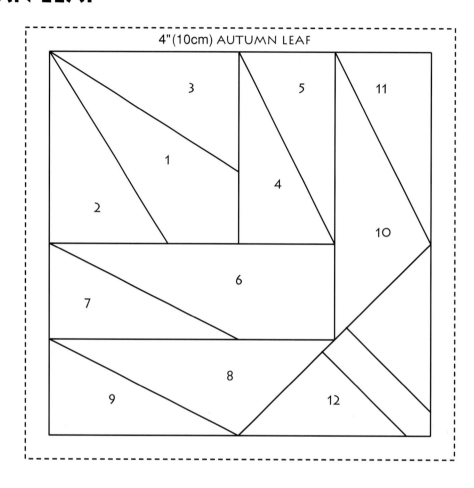

4"(10cm) AUTUMN LEAF

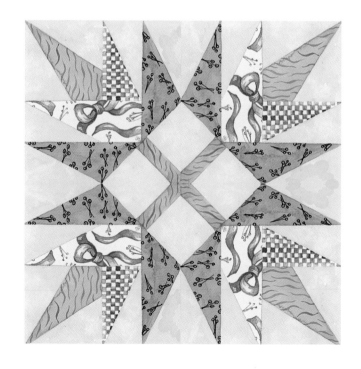

BIRD OF PARADISE FLOWER

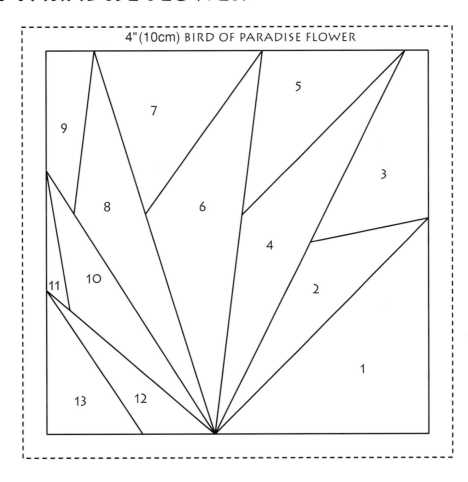

4"(10cm) BIRD OF PARADISE FLOWER

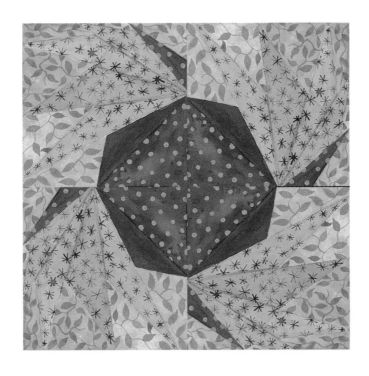

CACTUS FLOWER

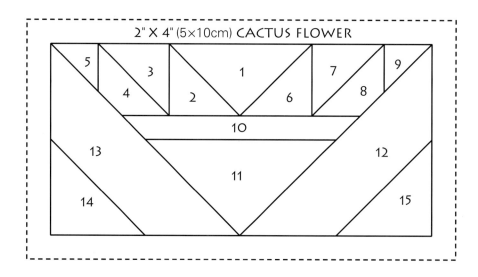

2" X 4" (5×10cm) CACTUS FLOWER

5 3 1 7 9
4 2 6 8
10
13 12
11
14 15

CORNER ROSE

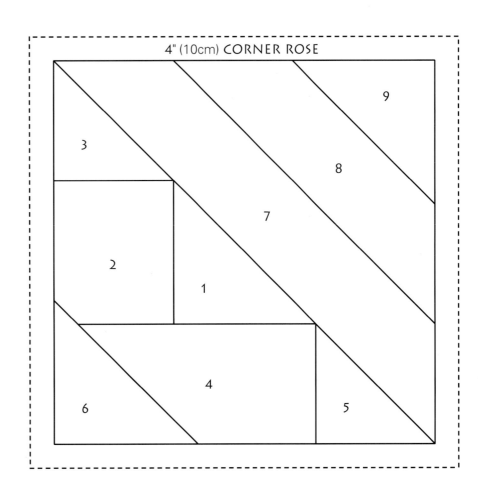

4" (10cm) CORNER ROSE

POTTED PLANT

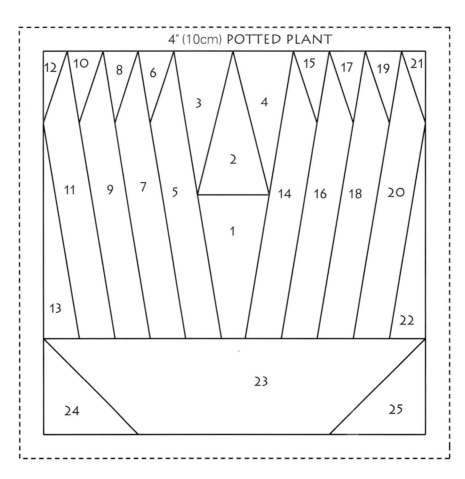

4" (10cm) POTTED PLANT

WATER LILY

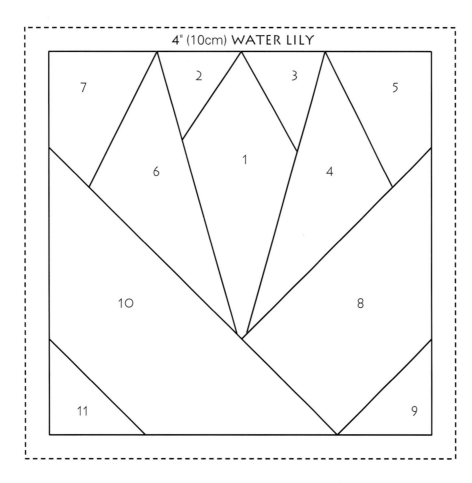

4" (10cm) WATER LILY

SPIKE FLOWER

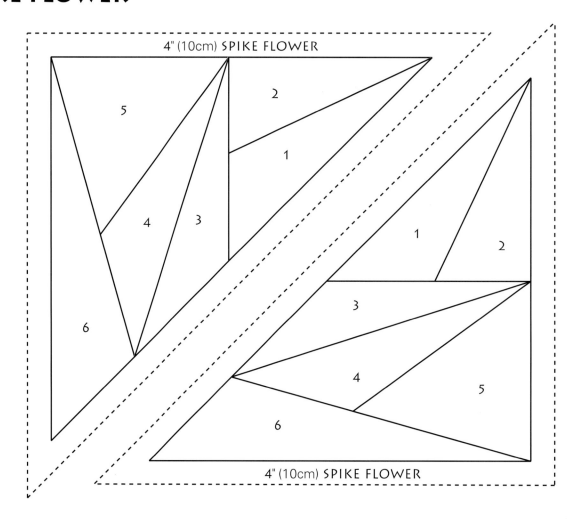

4" (10cm) SPIKE FLOWER

4" (10cm) SPIKE FLOWER

LEAF BUD

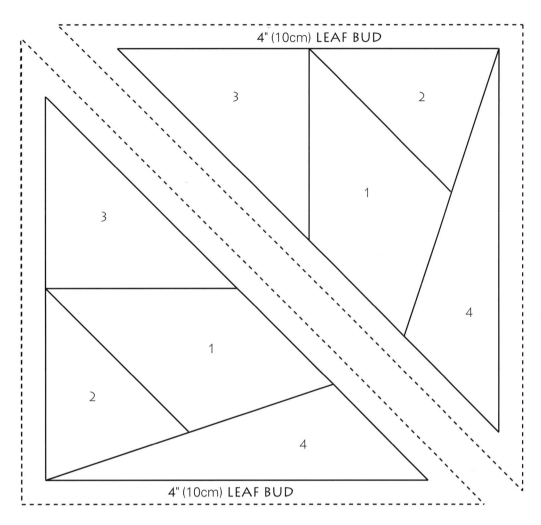

4" (10cm) LEAF BUD

4" (10cm) LEAF BUD

SHARP LEAF

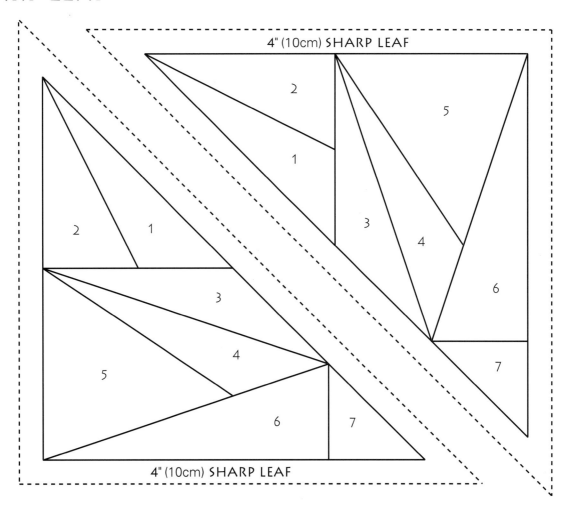

4" (10cm) SHARP LEAF

4" (10cm) SHARP LEAF

SPRING BUD

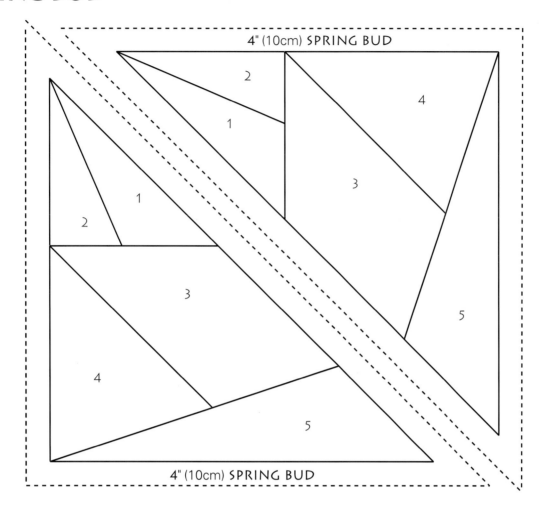

4" (10cm) SPRING BUD

4" (10cm) SPRING BUD

APPLE TREES

2" X 4" (5×10cm) SHORT APPLE TREE

2" X 4" (5×10cm) TALL APPLE TREE

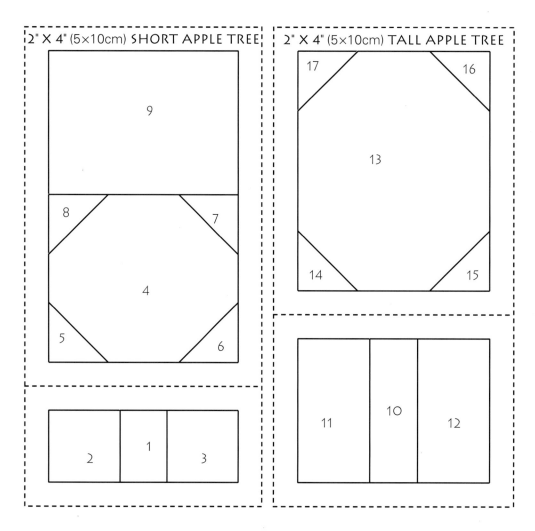

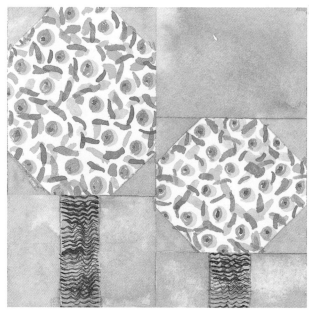

FRUITS AND VEGETABLES

Use some or all of these tasty blocks to make a colorful quilt with a garden theme that will look good enough to eat!

PEA POD ◆

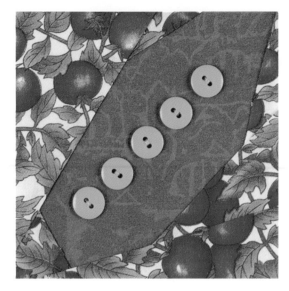

Like fresh peas picked right from the garden—choose bright buttons for these peas, or appliqué small circles of felt, wool, or ultrasuede.

CARROT ◆◆◆

Crisp and sweet, the first carrots of the summer—the perfect orange print will make your mouth water.

WATERMELON ◆

Soft and sweet, watermelon is summer's best fruit—color your watermelon red for realism and enjoy its refreshment.

PEAR ◆◆◆

Pear fruits so luscious you can almost smell them—enjoy coloring this one in greens and yellows.

SEED PACKET ◆

Use this framing foundation to set any of these patterns, or resize the flower patterns to three-inch squares and use this block to achieve movement in your garden.

CHERRIES ◆◆◆

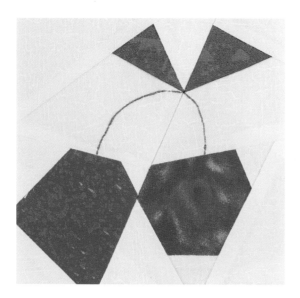

Fruit fresh straight from the tree—choose two different red prints to give your cherry bunch some dimensional appeal.

PEA POD

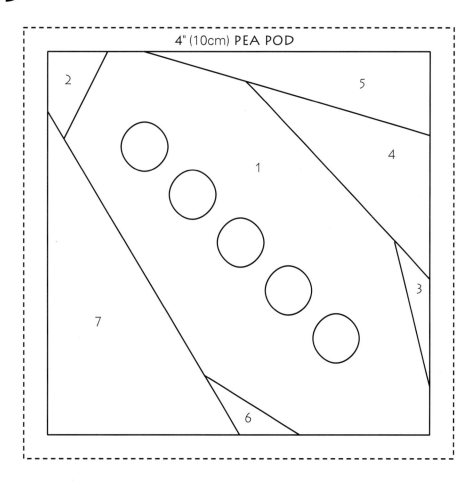

4" (10cm) PEA POD

2

5

1

4

3

7

6

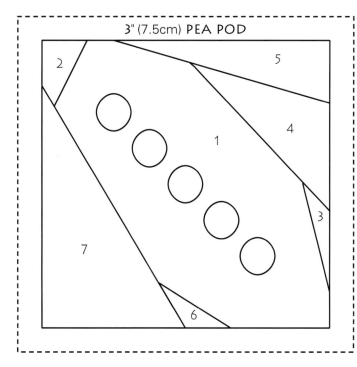

3" (7.5cm) PEA POD

2

5

1

4

3

7

6

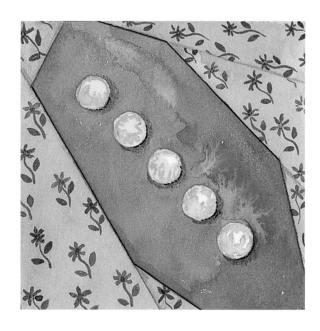

CARROT

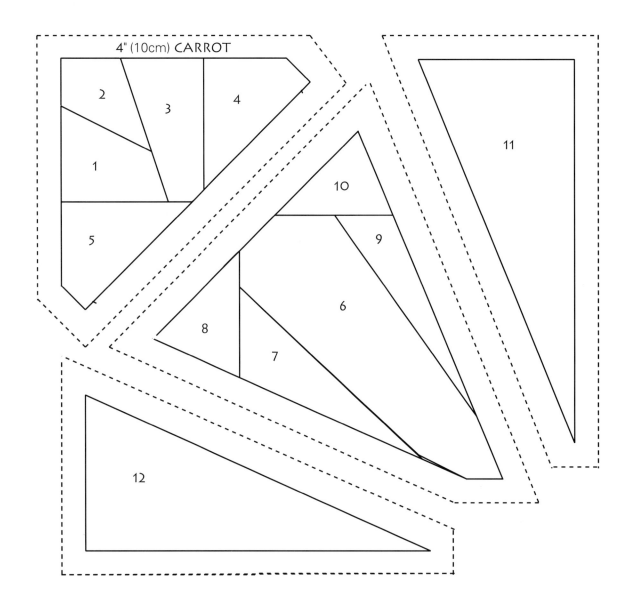

4" (10cm) CARROT

CARROT (CONTINUED)

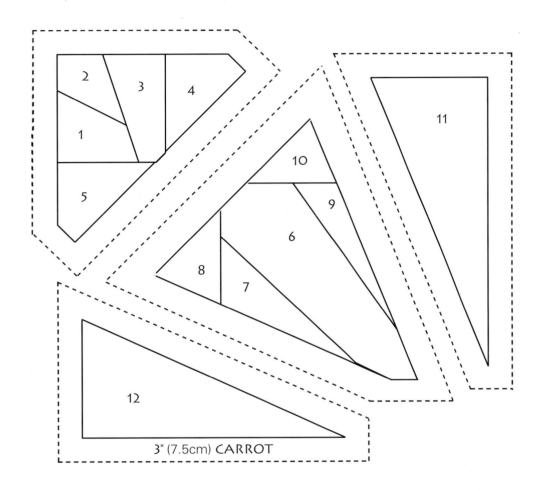

3" (7.5cm) CARROT

WATERMELON

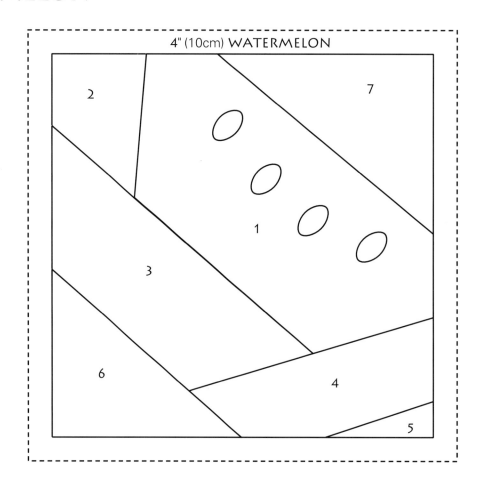

4" (10cm) WATERMELON

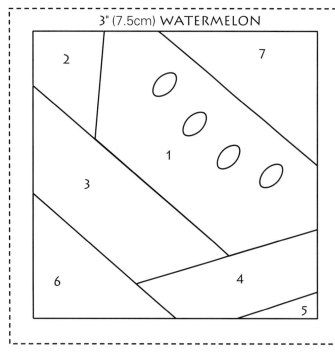

3" (7.5cm) WATERMELON

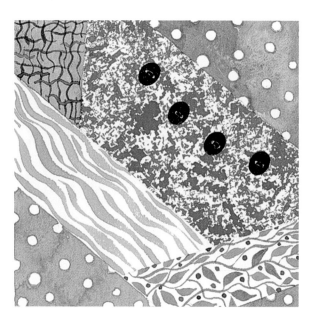

PEAR

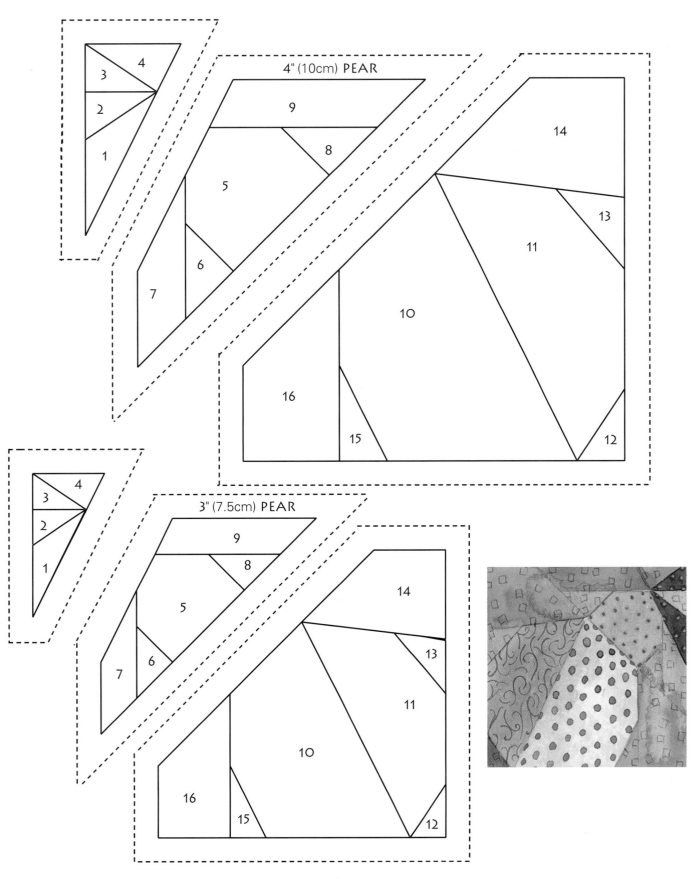

4" (10cm) PEAR

3" (7.5cm) PEAR

CHERRIES

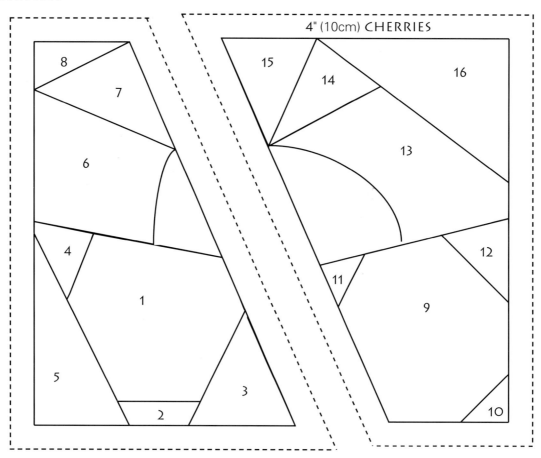

4" (10cm) CHERRIES

EMBROIDER OR INK STEMS

3" (7.5cm) CHERRIES

SEED PACKET

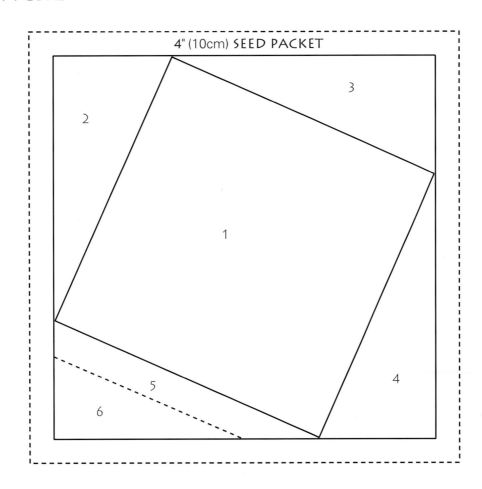

4" (10cm) SEED PACKET

ANIMALS

A playful animal will give your quilt lots of energy. These little critters will work on quilts with various themes.

BUTTERFLY I ◆◆

Pausing to spread its wings for your admiration, this butterfly can be made up in fabric prints or solids.

BUTTERFLY II ◆

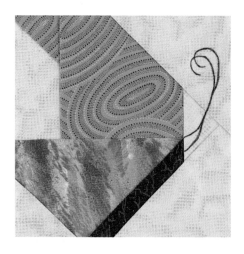

Make this butterfly in many colors and draw antennae in with permanent marker.

BUNNY ◆◆◆

Every perfect garden needs a bunny to remind the gardener how special her work really is. Use a button for your bunny's eye.

BIRD ◆◆

This bird will search out beetles or grubs in your garden. Give it plumage with real colors or in festival fantasy arrays—it's your garden! Draw legs with permanent marker and use a button for the eye.

FLYING BIRD ◆◆◆

Every garden needs pert (bug eating!) wrens and bluebirds to be complete. Let this one flit around on your next fabric garden.

FISH I ◆

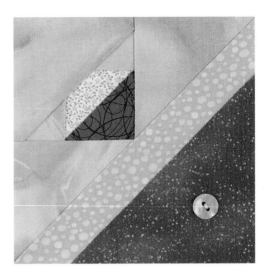

This fish curiously pokes into all corners of the lily pond. Give it good eyes for a more striking effect—they can be buttons, embroidery, paint, or appliqué.

GARDEN TOAD ◆◆

This sweet toad is so charming made up in different ways—every garden needs at least one to take care of those minor pesky insect annoyances and to bring good luck. Use a button for the eye.

FISH II ◆

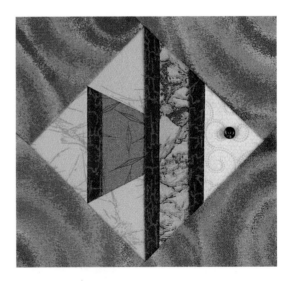

Choose the frame fabric for this fish carefully and have fun dressing it up or down with different fabrics for the stripes. A school of these flitting about the garden pond will ensure a lively effect.

BUTTERFLY I

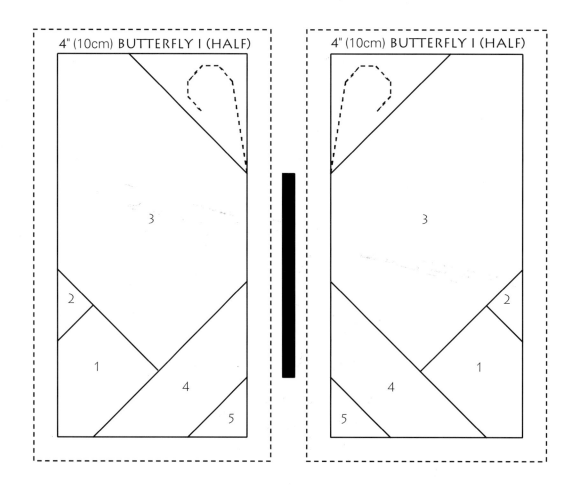

4" (10cm) BUTTERFLY I (HALF)

4" (10cm) BUTTERFLY I (HALF)

INSERT BLACK PIPING FOR BODY AS YOU SEAM TOGETHER HALVES; ANTENNAE CAN BE INKED WITH PIGMA PERMANENT PENS OR EMBROIDERED ON AFTER FOUNDATION REMOVAL

BUTTERFLY II

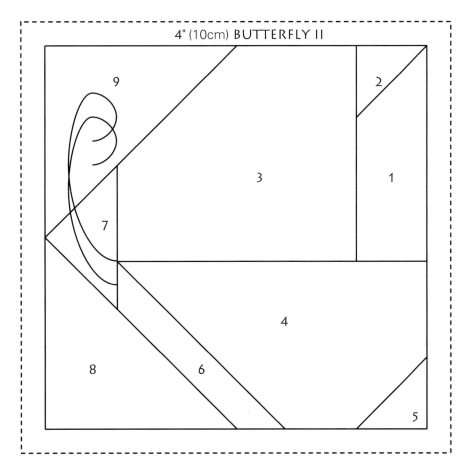

4" (10cm) BUTTERFLY II

ANTENNAE CAN BE INKED OR EMBROIDERED AFTER BLOCK ASSEMBLY

BUNNY

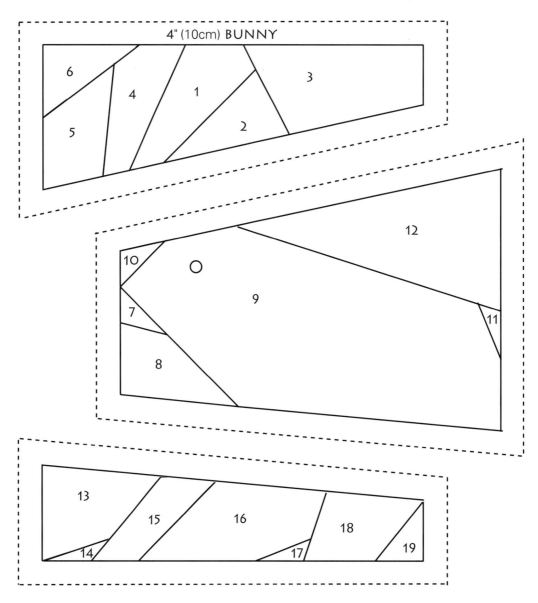

4" (10cm) BUNNY

6

4

1

3

5

2

10

12

O

9

7

11

8

13

15

16

18

14

17

19

BIRD

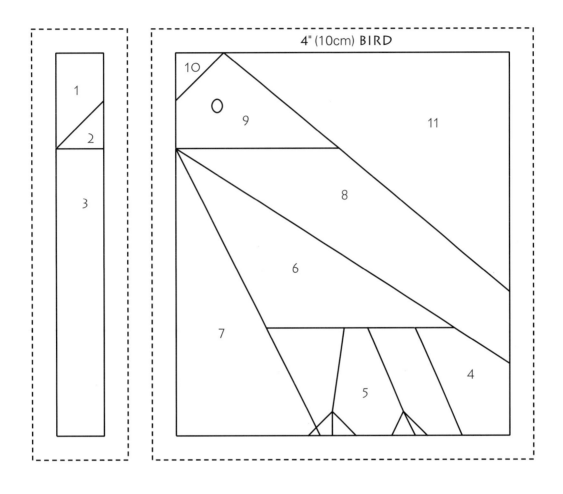

4" (10cm) BIRD

1
2
3

10
9
8
11
6
7
5
4

FLYING BIRD

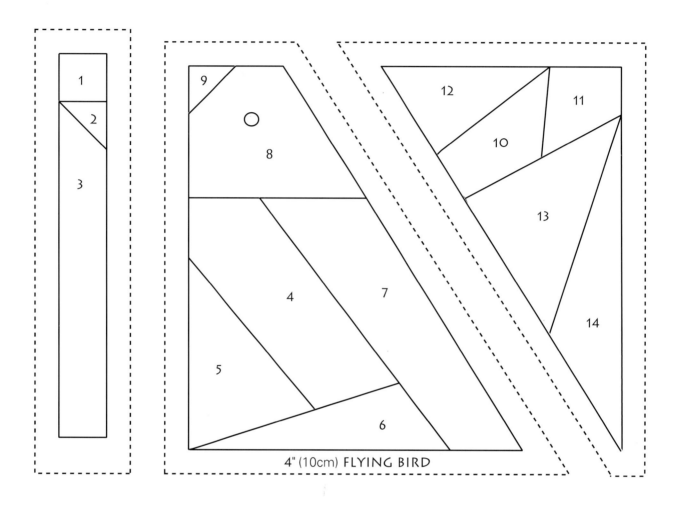

4" (10cm) FLYING BIRD

GARDEN TOAD

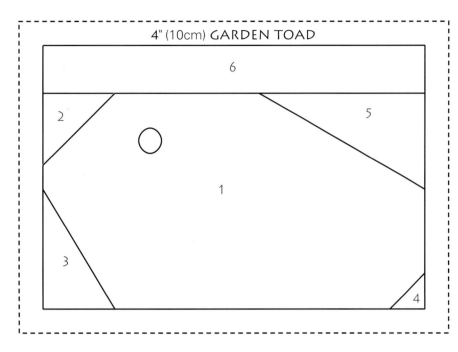

4" (10cm) GARDEN TOAD

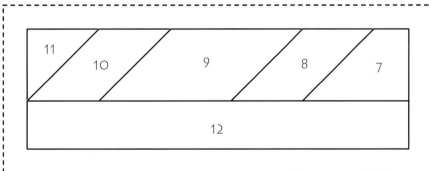

FISH I

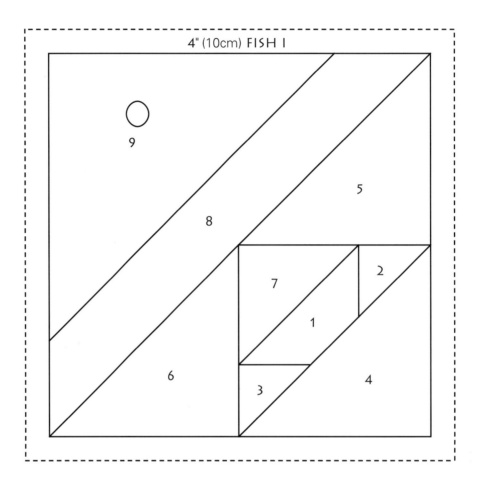

4" (10cm) FISH I

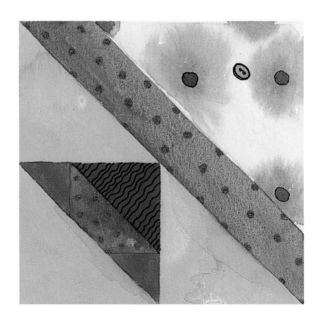

FISH II

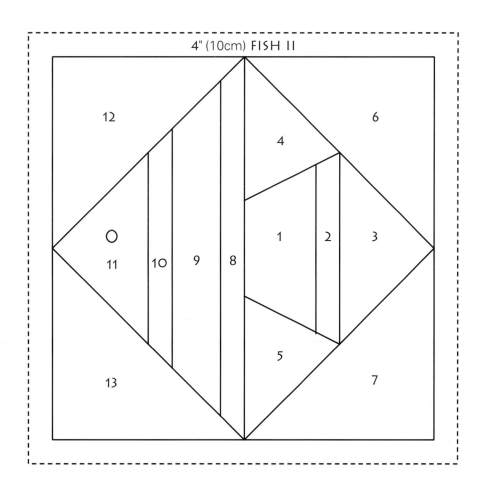

4" (10cm) FISH II

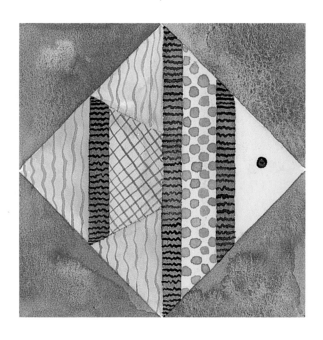

GARDEN ACCESSORIES

Round out your garden-themed quilt with accessories that are essential to any garden, whether as a tool or decoration.

JAPANESE LANTERN ♦♦

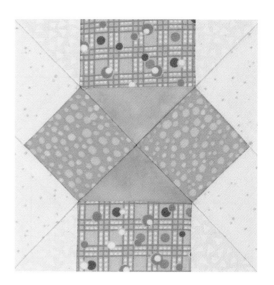

This pattern takes more work than some but yields a perfect party adornment. Enhance your fantasy-fabric get-together with a string of lights shining brightly.

PICKET FENCE ♦

Making the subunits for this fence is slightly more trouble than the other borders we have given in this book...but picket fences are appealing backdrops for romantic gardens. Choose your fabrics with pleasure for exactly the effect you want.

WHIRLIGIG ♦♦

This pattern is an adaption of a traditional block with lots of movement. Put a few of these in among your flowers for energy or make a whole quilt in a whirl.

BIRD FEEDER ◆

Keep your feeder filled with good seed and the birds will repay you with their sweet songs all summer. Have fun making this feeder as realistic or fanciful as you like.

GARDEN LIGHT ◆

Bright lanterns glowing in the twilight make for a romantic garden. Make yours in realistic or exotic fabrics to suit your fancy.

FRUIT BOWL ◆

This is a very simple pattern and will work best with an interesting background fabric. Set it on point for a more realistic effect. You can fill the basket with buttons, embroidery, or 3-D appliqué flowers.

MAY BASKET ◆

This simple traditional basket will serve for fruit or flower picking. Choose a special background print to enhance its beauty.

WATERING CAN ◆◆◆

Watering by hand is a pleasant task for the gardener. Choose a fabric you enjoy for this important gardener's standby—green to match the foliage or electric neon so you won't forget to bring it home.

BIRDHOUSE ◆◆

This is an easy block to make despite the need for subunit assembly. Have lots of fun choosing an assortment of fabrics for a bird city in your garden.

SPADE ◆◆

An indispensable garden tool, the spade makes a wonderful icon for the rewards of hard labor. This one will fit into the corner of your fabric garden (which needs no spadework to bloom).

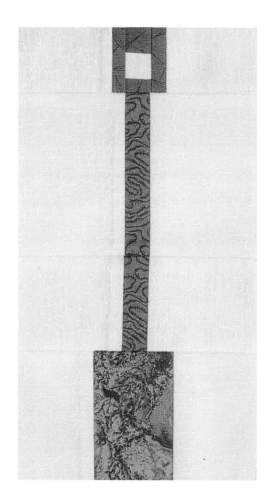

JAPANESE LANTERN

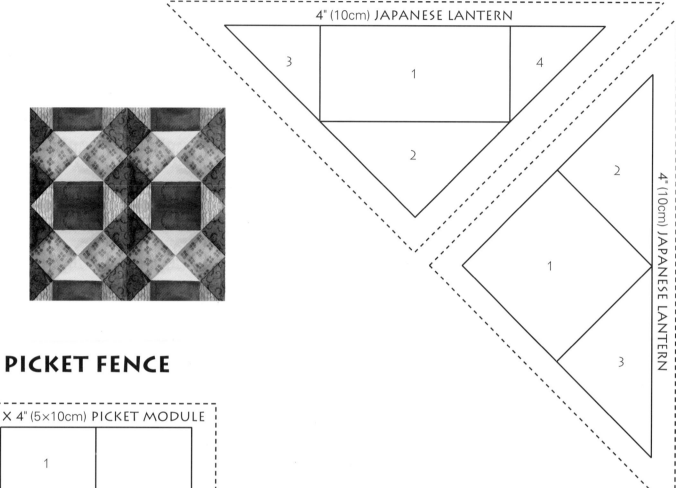

4" (10cm) JAPANESE LANTERN

4" (10cm) JAPANESE LANTERN

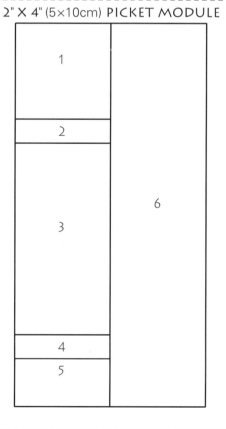

PICKET FENCE

2" X 4" (5×10cm) PICKET MODULE

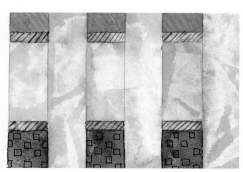

WHIRLIGIG

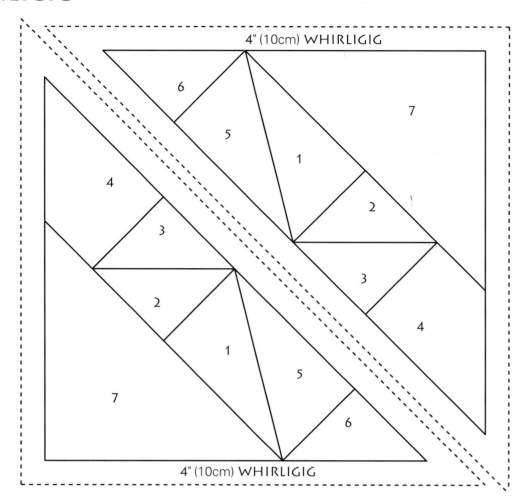

4" (10cm) WHIRLIGIG

BIRD FEEDER

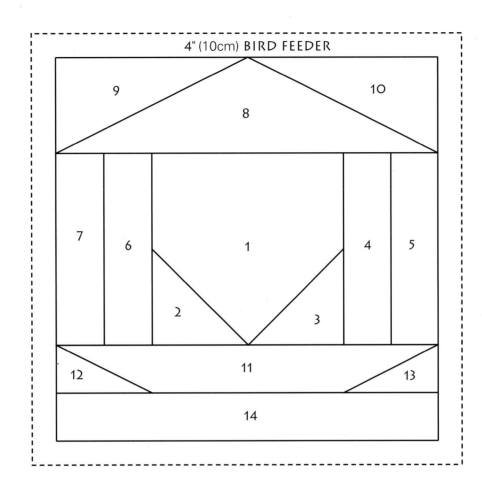

4" (10cm) BIRD FEEDER

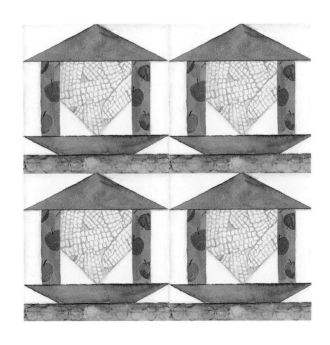

FRUIT BOWL

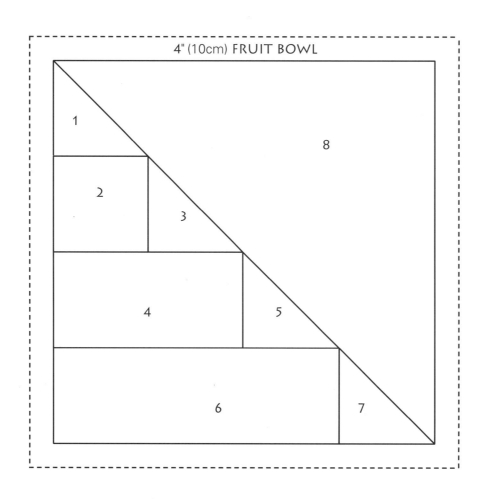

4" (10cm) FRUIT BOWL

GARDEN LIGHT

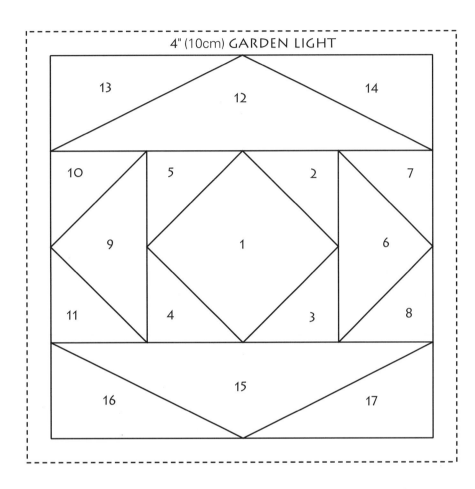

4" (10cm) GARDEN LIGHT

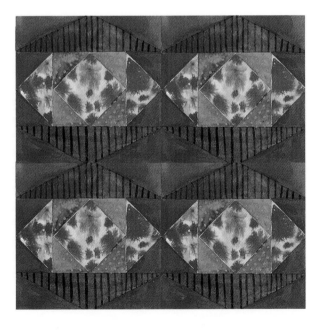

GARDEN LIGHT

MAY BASKET

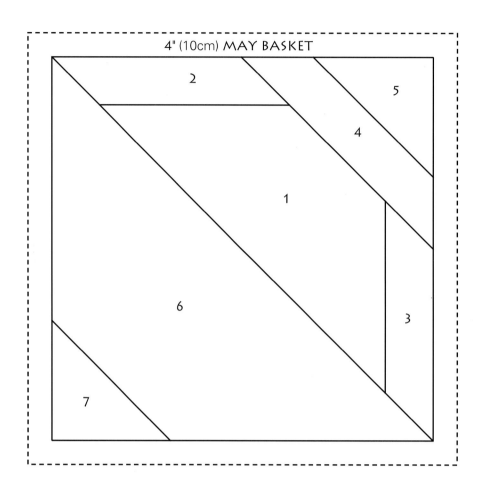

4" (10cm) MAY BASKET

WATERING CAN

4" (10cm) WATERING CAN

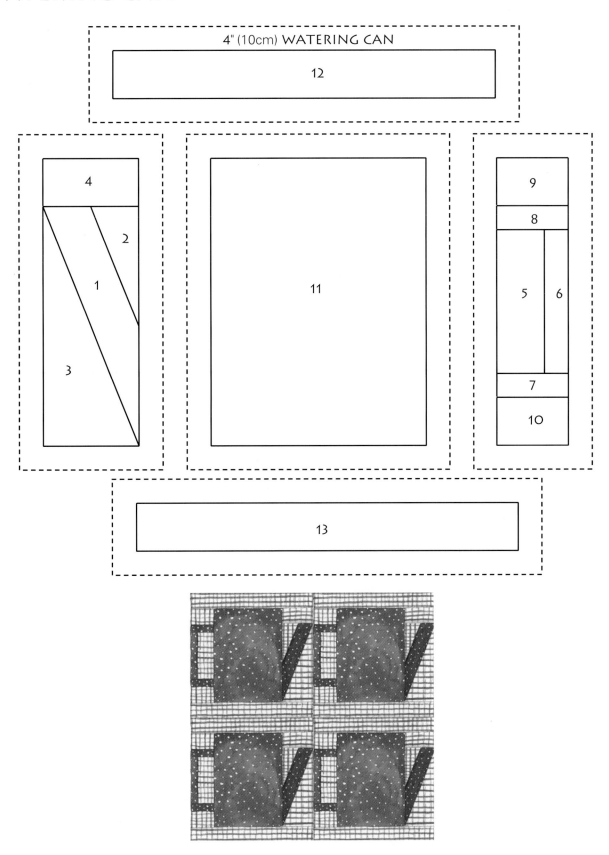

BIRDHOUSE

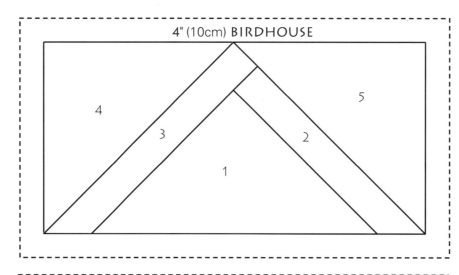

4" (10cm) BIRDHOUSE

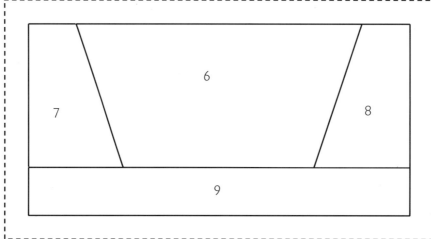

USE ¾" DIAMETER BUTTON FOR ENTRY HOLE

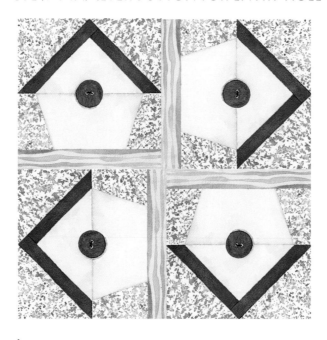

SPADE

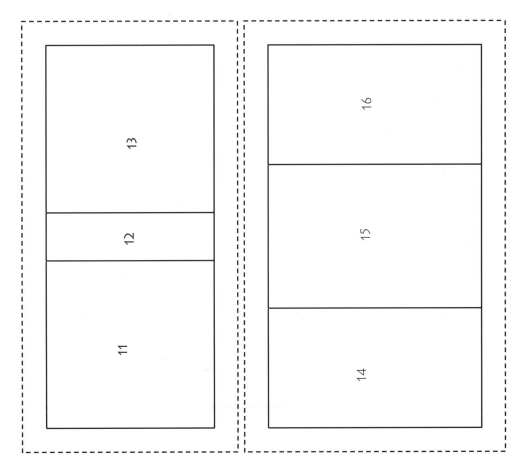

4" X 8" (10×20.5cm) GARDEN SPADE

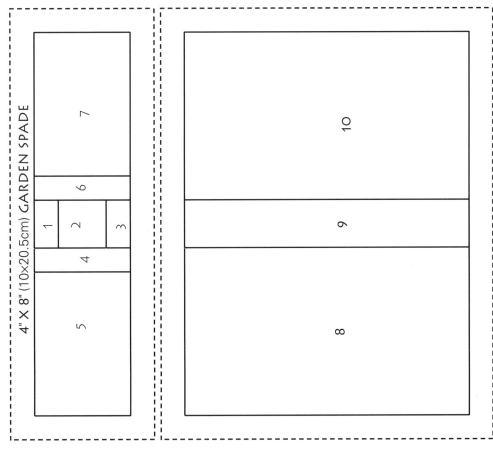

LANDSCAPES

These lovely scenic blocks make for beautiful backdrops in a quilt that promotes serenity.

SUNRISE OVER MOUNTAIN LAKE ◆

This landscape is more elaborate than the others but still very easy to construct. Make different times of day or seasons of the year for an effective quilt.

GREEN WOODS ◆

This easy block evokes woodsy walks and silent green beauty. Put several together for your own secret fabric hideaway.

ROAD THROUGH THE WOODS ◆

Where does this road go? Mine heads into the hills to Grandma's house. Your fabric choices can make this a very seasonal block; maybe you would enjoy your own version of homecoming for every season of the year.

THE ROAD HOME ♦

Simpler than Road Through The Woods, this block evokes family visits to the country to see loved ones. Choose an assortment of prints to make this simple block heartwarming.

LAKE IN THE MOUNTAINS ♦

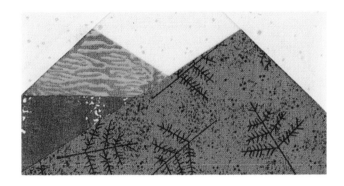

This small patchwork landscape can be used effectively as a border or as part of a larger landscape quilt. Enjoy choosing just the right print for the water and sky (be sure to consider using the back side of the sky print for the water surface).

FARAWAY VISTAS ♦

Create a simple small block of faraway mountains. Remember that the farthest mountains should be colored the lightest if you want a realistic effect. These small blocks can be arranged together in many ways.

MOUNTAIN LAKE ♦

Enjoy fitting this small landscape into your larger picture. You can enhance the mountains by choosing different prints.

MOUNTAIN SUNRISE ◆

Early morning mists rising off the mountains give the air a sweet fresh tang. The energy of your landscape will be affected strongly by your choice for sun fabric—pale fabrics will give a peaceful meditative quality to the morning, bright ones will lend vibrant energy to the start of the day. Or be daring and craft a beautiful mountain sunset instead.

CORNER SUNSHINE ◆◆

From soft early morning light to hot afternoon, this pattern will give your fabric garden life and energy in scrappy oranges and yellows...or in dramatic solids.

MOUNTAINS ◆

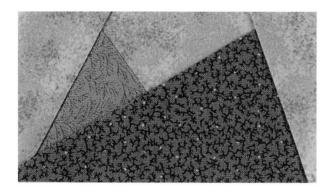

Combine this block with far vistas to make a dramatic horizon for your garden. Experiment with mountain colors and prints.

GREEN WOODS

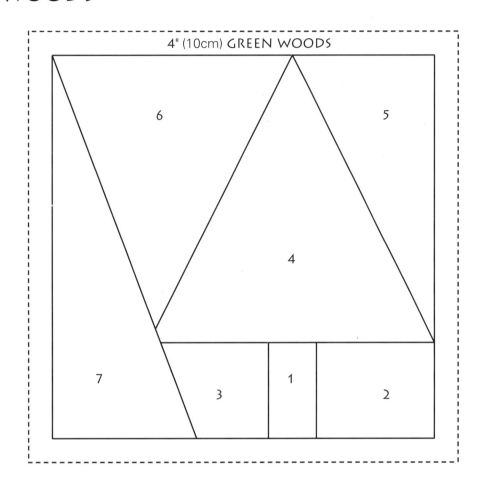

4" (10cm) GREEN WOODS

SUNRISE OVER MOUNTAIN LAKE

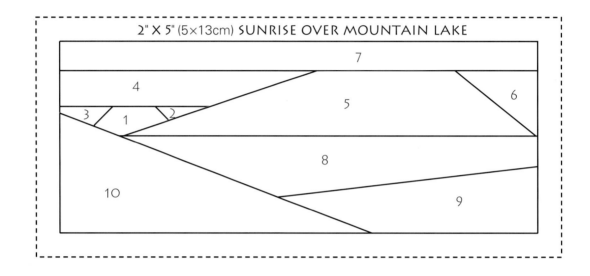

2" X 5" (5×13cm) SUNRISE OVER MOUNTAIN LAKE

ROAD THROUGH THE WOODS

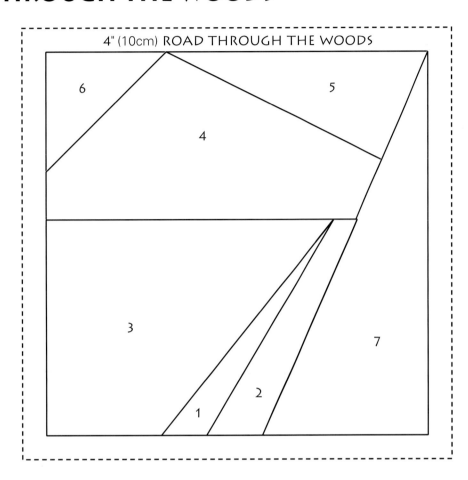

4" (10cm) ROAD THROUGH THE WOODS

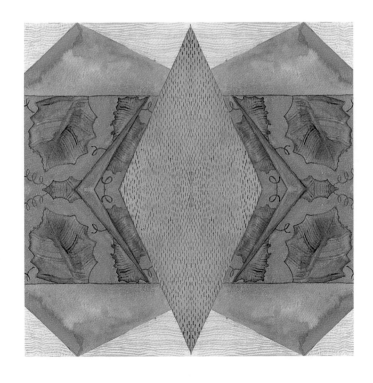

THE ROAD HOME

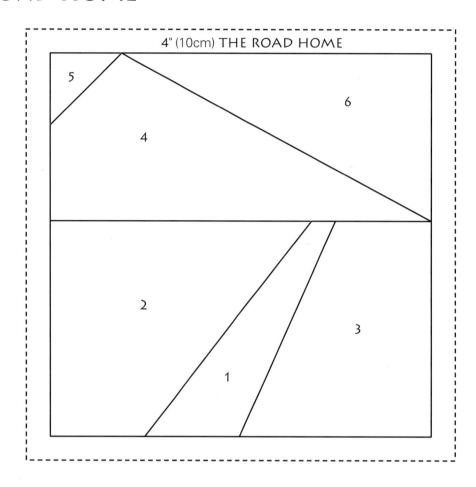

4" (10cm) THE ROAD HOME

FARAWAY VISTAS

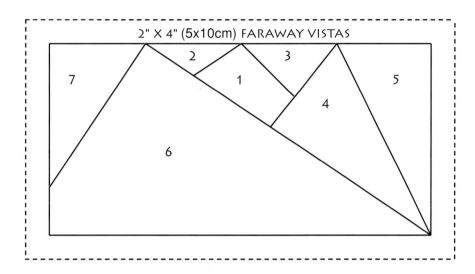

2" X 4" (5x10cm) FARAWAY VISTAS

LAKE IN THE MOUNTAINS

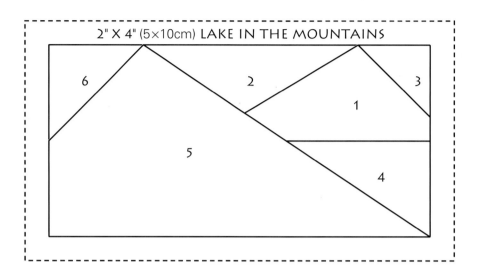

2" X 4" (5×10cm) LAKE IN THE MOUNTAINS

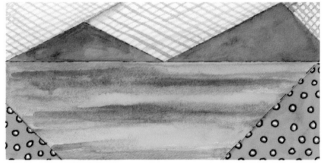

MOUNTAIN LAKE

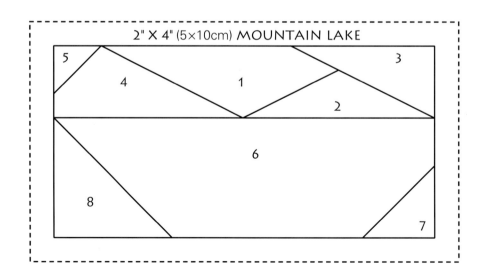

2" X 4" (5×10cm) MOUNTAIN LAKE

MOUNTAIN SUNRISE

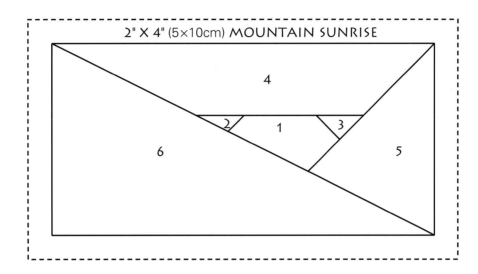

2" X 4" (5×10cm) MOUNTAIN SUNRISE

MOUNTAINS

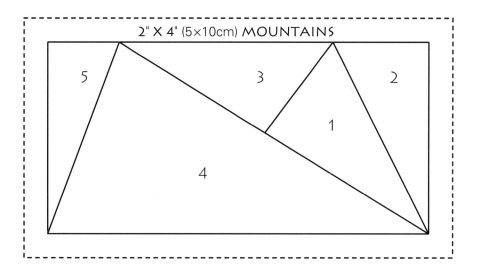

2" X 4" (5×10cm) MOUNTAINS

CORNER SUNSHINE

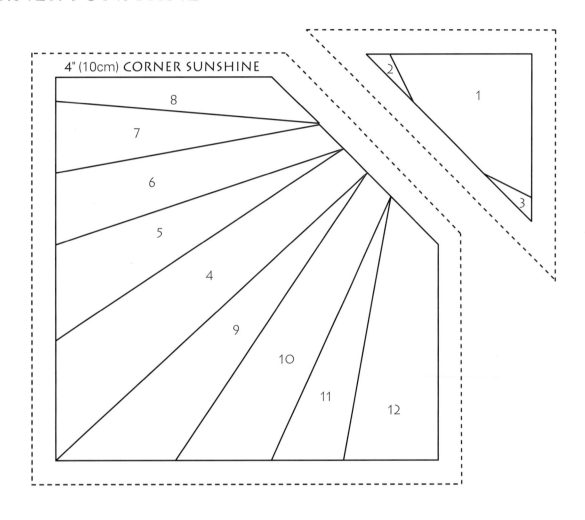

4" (10cm) CORNER SUNSHINE

STANDING HEARTS

Nothing symbolizes romance better than a heart. Use these blocks to make a special Valentine quilt.

LARGE UPRIGHT HEART ◆

Use brilliant fabrics with this simple heart pattern to make a memorable statement.

STRIPED HEART ◆

A gradation of colors will make a beautiful rainbow for this heart.

BRAIDED HEART ◆

Choose your fabrics thoughtfully to give this block that wrapped-in-love look.

CRAZY HEART ♦

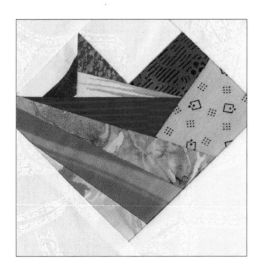

For an old-time crazy-quilt look, make this block on a fabric foundation using an assortment of silks, velvets, or lace. Embroider over seam lines for an authentic touch.

FLOWER OF LOVE HEART ♦

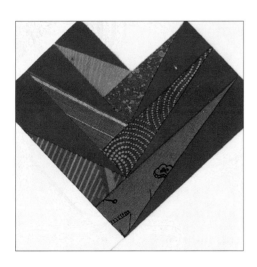

Some days we are all prickles and thorns, even to the ones we love. This heart block will make for a great apology.

BEATING HEART ♦

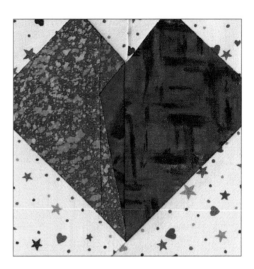

Two contrasting fabrics will make this heart appear to beat wildly.

PUZZLE HEART I ♦

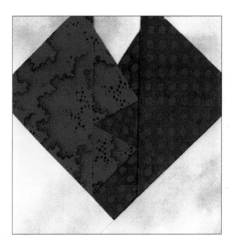

Remember those separating charms you used to share with your most special friends? Put yours back together in this block.

DOUBLE HEART ♦ ♦

Keep your loved one safe in your heart. Choose fabrics with colors or prints that hold special meaning to each of you and that have good contrast.

HEART AND HOME ♦ ♦

Love of hearth and home is basic to security and happiness. Express your feelings with this pattern.

HEART FRAME BLOCK ♦ ♦

When you use solid fabric for the internal square, this block is a good one for calligraphy and poetry.

PATRIOT AT HEART ♦ ♦

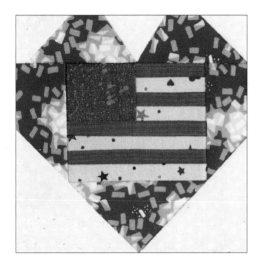

Your strong patriotic feelings will shine through with this easy pattern.

HEAD OVER HEELS ♦ ♦ ♦

Falling in love is a dizzying experience, but exciting all the same. Use joyful colors in this pattern for a glorious result.

KEY TO MY HEART ♦ ♦

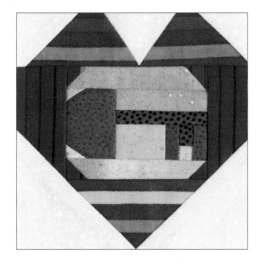

Give the key to your heart to your Valentine this year with this special block.

LARGE UPRIGHT HEART

Creative options

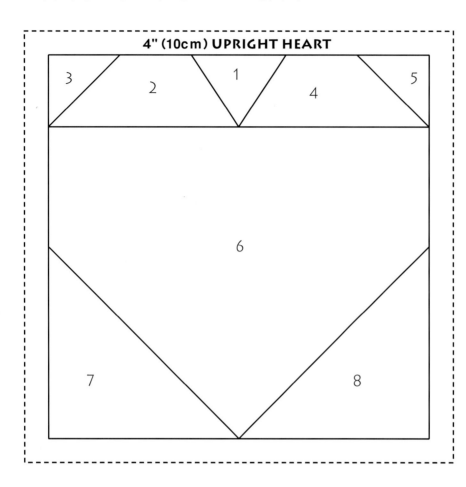

4" (10cm) UPRIGHT HEART

3   2   1   4   5

6

7   8

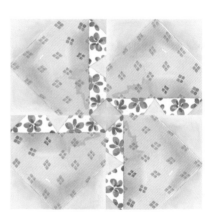

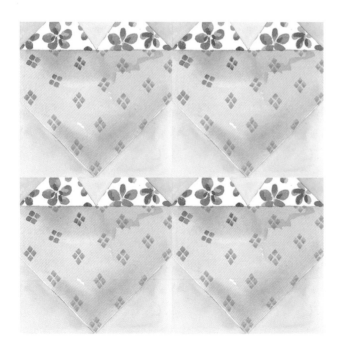

STRIPED HEART

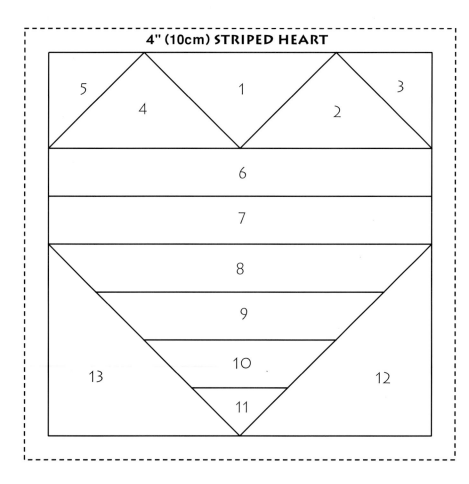

4" (10cm) STRIPED HEART

5 1 3
4 2
6
7
8
9
10
13 12
11

Creative options

BRAIDED HEART

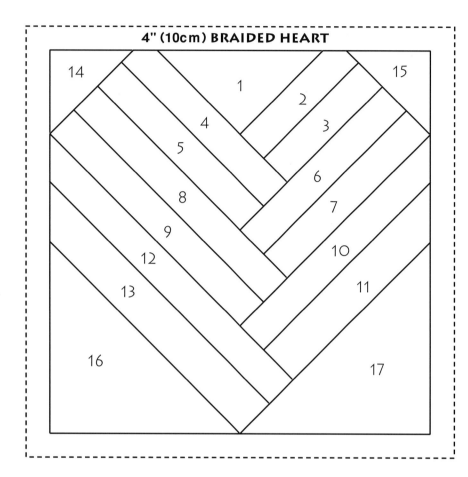

4" (10cm) BRAIDED HEART

14 15 1 2 4 3 5 6 8 7 9 10 12 11 13 16 17

Creative options

CRAZY HEART

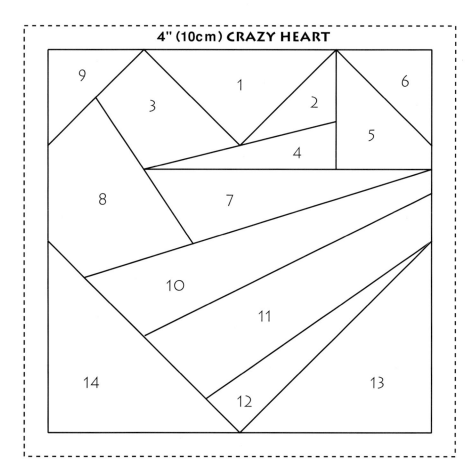

4" (10cm) CRAZY HEART

Creative options

FLOWER OF LOVE HEART

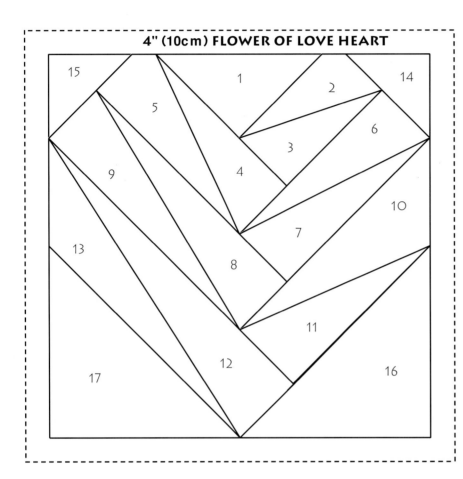

4" (10cm) FLOWER OF LOVE HEART

15 · 1 · 2 · 14 · 5 · 6 · 3 · 4 · 9 · 7 · 10 · 8 · 13 · 11 · 12 · 17 · 16

Creative options

BEATING HEART

Creative options

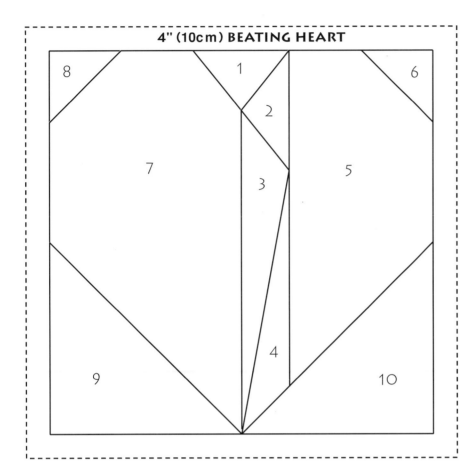

4" (10cm) BEATING HEART

8

1

6

2

7

3

5

4

9

10

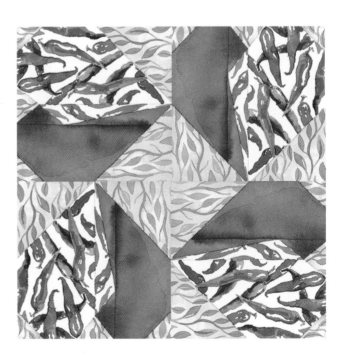

PUZZLE HEART I

Creative options

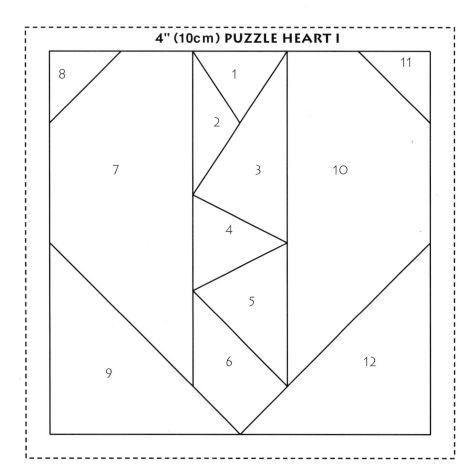

4" (10cm) PUZZLE HEART I

8
11
1
2
7
3
10
4
5
9
6
12

DOUBLE HEART

Creative options

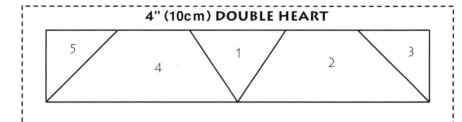

4" (10cm) DOUBLE HEART

5   4   1   2   3

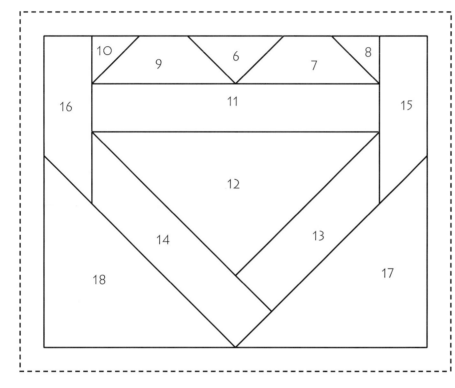

10   9   6   7   8

16   11   15

12

14   13

18   17

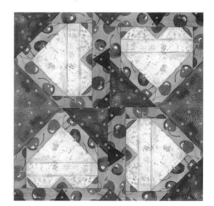

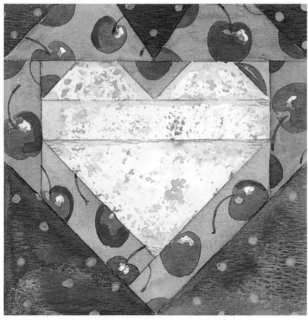

HEART FRAME BLOCK

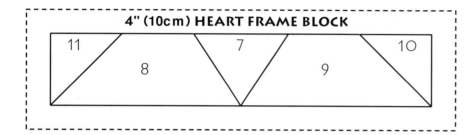

4" (10cm) HEART FRAME BLOCK

11 7 10
8 9

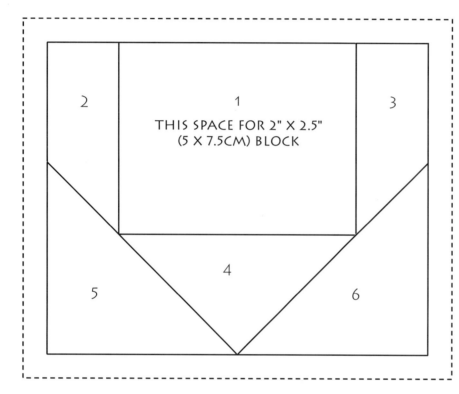

2 1 3

THIS SPACE FOR 2" X 2.5"
(5 X 7.5CM) BLOCK

4

5 6

THIS BLOCK CAN BE USED TO FEATURE A SPECIAL FABRIC MOTIF, LACE, EMBROIDERY, LETTER MESSAGE, OR PHOTO TRANSFER. YOU CAN USE THE INSERTION PATTERNS ON PAGES 38–39, OR THE SCRIPT ALPHABET ON PAGE 23 TO SEND A SPECIAL MESSAGE.

Creative options

HEART AND HOME
(INSERTION PATTERN)

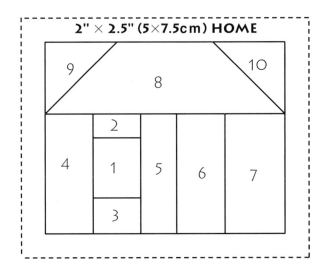

2" × 2.5" (5×7.5cm) HOME

Suggested use in Heart Frame (page 180)

PATRIOT AT HEART
(INSERTION PATTERN)

2" × 2.5" (5×7.5cm) PATRIOT AT HEART

Suggested use in Heart Frame (page 170)

KEY TO MY HEART
(INSERTION PATTERN)

2" X 2.5" (5X7.5cm) KEY TO MY HEART

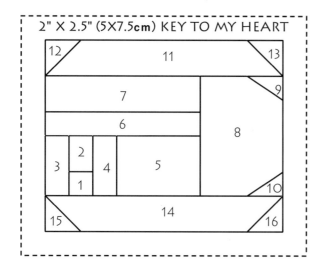

Suggested use in Heart Frame (page 180)

Creative options

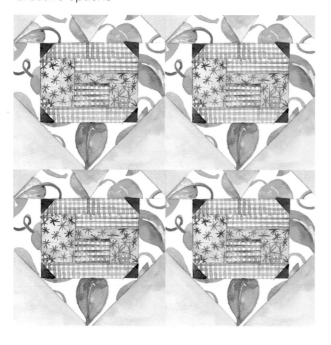

HEAD OVER HEELS

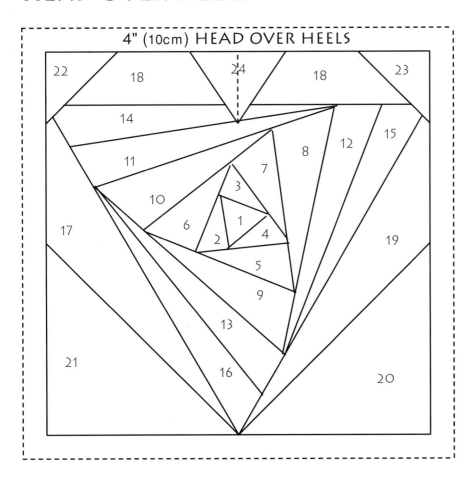

4" (10cm) HEAD OVER HEELS

SEW PIECE 18 AS ONE STRIP. SEW PIECE 24 ON TOP OF PIECES 14 AND 18. AFTER SEWING PIECE 24, DOTTED LINE SHOWS PLACEMENT OF FOLD WHEN PRESSING PIECE UPWARD; TRIM EXCESS FABRIC.

NOTE: TO SEW PIECE 24, SEE PAGE 19 FOR "STITCH AND TUCK TRICK."

Creative option

HEARTS ON POINT

These slanted hearts will create visual interest and fun in your next quilt.

HEARTTHROB ◆

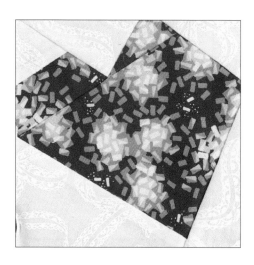

Use dazzling colors to make a quilt bursting with energy and excitement for your heartthrob.

DIAGONAL HEART ◆

This simple pattern is smashing when made in a wide range of colors and patterns: try Amish brights, country florals, hand-dyed solids, or wild, contemporary prints.

DIAGONAL HEART FRAME ◆

You can spell out your special Valentine message in this special heart frame.

DIAGONAL STRIPED HEART ◆ ◆

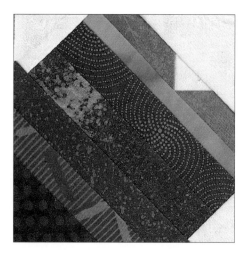

Irregular strips allow for a number of different fabric tricks. Consider sewing charms or tiny prairie points onto this block.

DIAGONAL BRAIDED
HEART ◆◆

Try shading fabrics from dark to light in either direction for a memorable result in this pattern.

DIAGONAL DOUBLE
HEART ◆◆

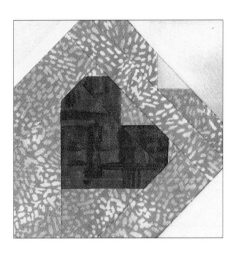

Fabrics with good contrast will give the best results when making this block for someone you hold dear.

DIAGONAL CRAZY
HEART ◆◆

The patch shapes in this pattern may be embellished with silk ribbon or floss embroidery, painting, or calligraphy. Let your imagination run wild and create a truly striking crazy quilt.

PUZZLE HEART II ◆ ◆

Like medieval betrothal rings that were sometimes made as interlocking puzzle pairs, this pattern will relay a message of togetherness with love.

STRING OF HEARTS ◆ ◆ ◆

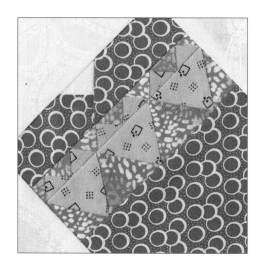

Show someone just how much you love him or her with this pattern created from multiple hearts.

HEARTTHROB

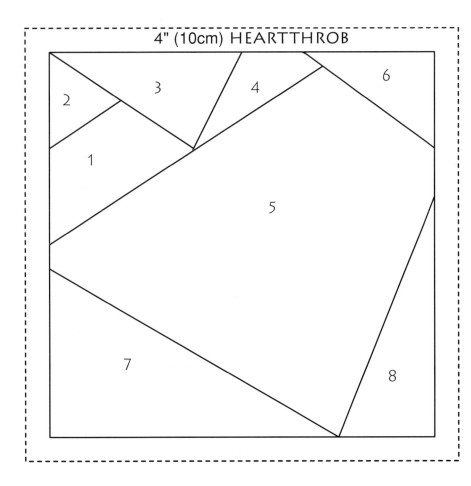

4" (10cm) HEARTTHROB

2 3 4 6
1
5
7 8

Creative options

DIAGONAL HEART

Creative options

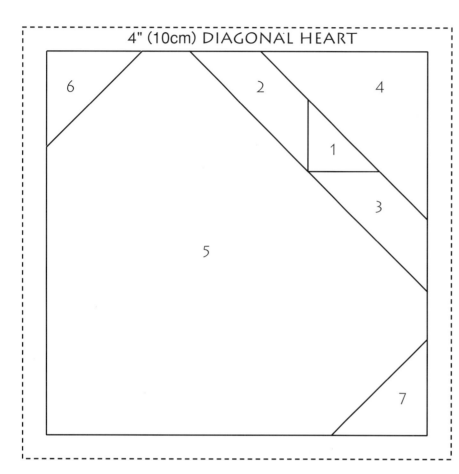

4" (10cm) DIAGONAL HEART

6

2

4

1

3

5

7

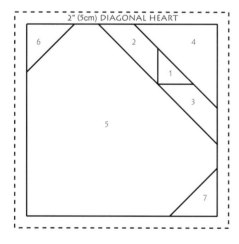

2" (5cm) DIAGONAL HEART

6

2

4

1

3

5

7

DIAGONAL HEART FRAME

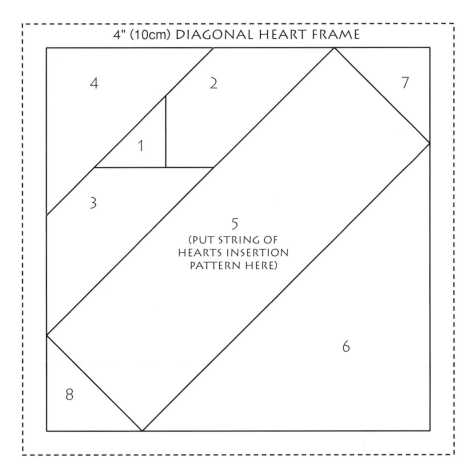

4" (10cm) DIAGONAL HEART FRAME

4 2 7

1

3

5
(PUT STRING OF
HEARTS INSERTION
PATTERN HERE)

6

8

Creative options

DIAGONAL STRIPED HEART

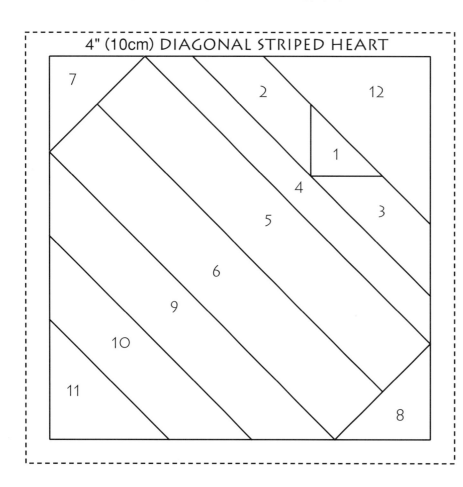

4" (10cm) DIAGONAL STRIPED HEART

7

2   12

1

4

3

5

6

9

10

11

8

Creative options

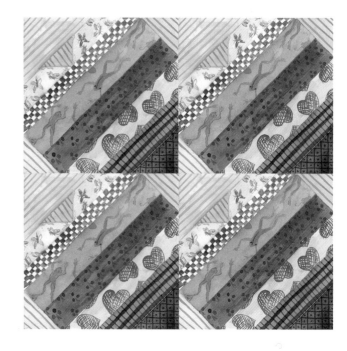

DIAGONAL BRAIDED HEART

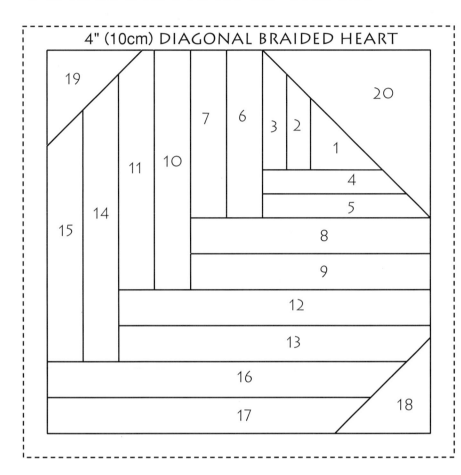

4" (10cm) DIAGONAL BRAIDED HEART

Creative options

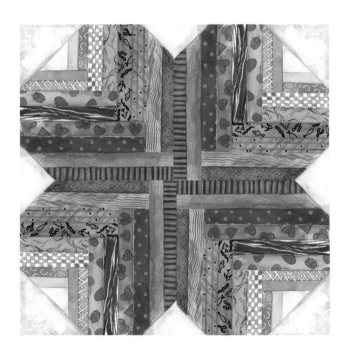

DIAGONAL CRAZY HEART

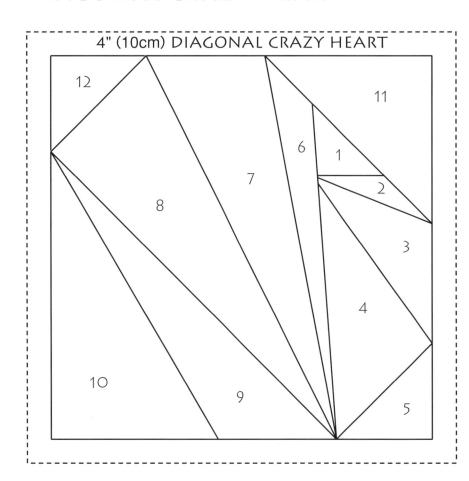

4" (10cm) DIAGONAL CRAZY HEART

Creative options

DIAGONAL DOUBLE HEART

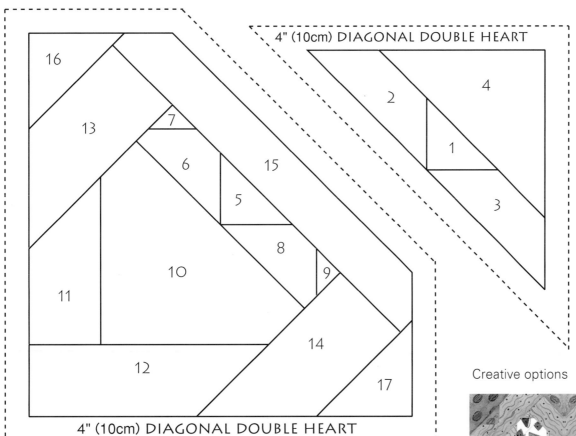

4" (10cm) DIAGONAL DOUBLE HEART

4" (10cm) DIAGONAL DOUBLE HEART

Creative options

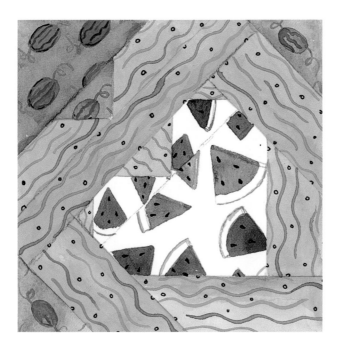

PUZZLE HEART II

Creative options

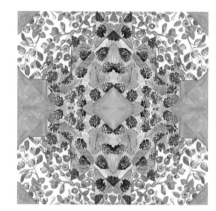

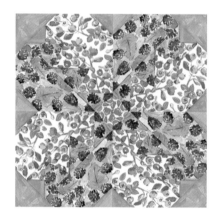

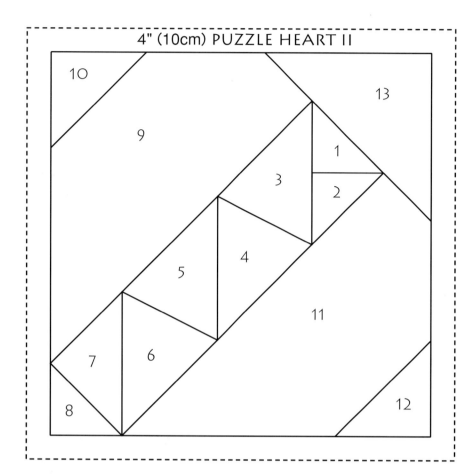

4" (10cm) PUZZLE HEART II

10

13

9

1

3

2

4

5

11

7

6

8

12

STRING OF HEARTS

(INSERTION PATTERN)

Creative options

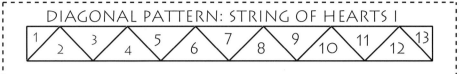

DIAGONAL PATTERN: STRING OF HEARTS I

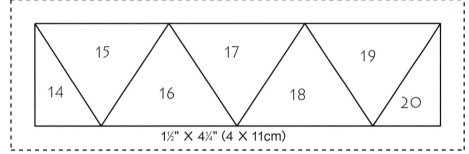

1½" X 4¼" (4 X 11cm)

Suggested use in Diagonal Heart Frame (page 189)

FLOWERS AND ANIMAL FRIENDS

Flowers, butterflies, and cuddly animals always conjure up images of romance. Decorate your Valentines with these blocks, or make a sweet sampler for a friend.

FLOWER BASKET ◆

Sash fabrics make this basket special. "Fill" the basket with buttons or yo-yos.

RESURRECTION BUTTERFLY ◆ ◆

A dramatic butterfly pattern, this one looks striking when made with either Amish or hand-dyed solid fabrics.

LOVE BIRD ◆ ◆

This sweet little bird is adorable and so easy to make. Use a favorite button for the eye.

SCOTTIE DOG ♦ ♦

With a loyal heart, this little dog makes a great accent to a playful quilt.

ROSE IN BLOOM ♦ ♦

Spiraling petals lead your eyes into the heart of this flower. Varying patterns and colors will help make your own special rose garden.

PLAYFUL KITTY ♦ ♦

Every cat lover knows the joy that a frisky, furry friend can bring. Make this quilt for that special cat lover in your life.

FUCHSIA ♦ ♦

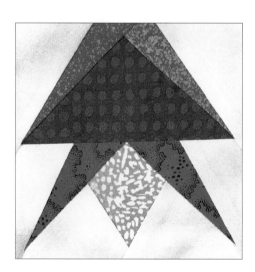

Bright with color, the fuchsia blossom dazzles the eye. Let this pattern sizzle in your fabric garden.

FANTASY VINE ◆ ◆

A series of these vine blocks can be arranged into any layout that works with diamond shapes.

HIDDEN FLOWER ◆ ◆

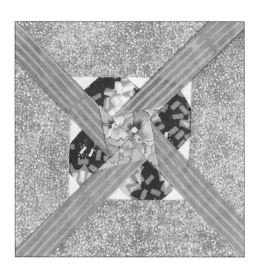

This is an adaptation of a traditional pattern with many different coloring possibilities. The resulting quilt's overall design will be full of energy and diagonal movement.

BUD AND BUTTERFLY ◆ ◆

Another traditional pattern, this block offers many color possibilities. Enjoy making butterflies flit around a garden of flowers.

BUTTERFLY III ◆ ◆ ◆

This fragile creature will grace your next flower garden in fabric.

ORIENTAL TULIP ◆◆◆

This stalwart flower can brighten your fabric gardens and carry your thoughts of love in a permanent display.

BASKET OF FLOWERS ◆◆◆

This traditional block is striking when made in contemporary fabrics. Send a small basket of cheerful flowers to a friend!

BROMELIAD FLOWER ◆◆◆

Full of spikes and bright colors, this block is easy to make and requires no seam matching to be brilliant.

FLOWER BASKET

Creative options

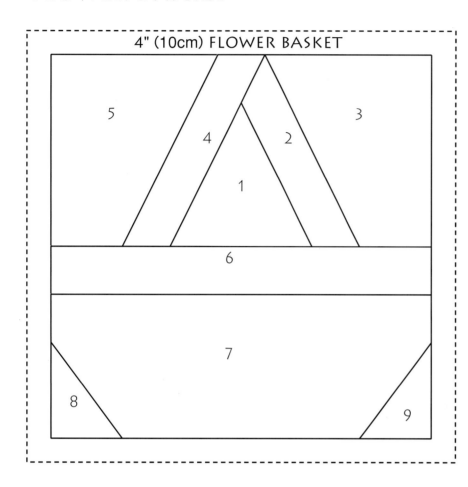

4" (10cm) FLOWER BASKET

5

4

3

2

1

6

7

8

9

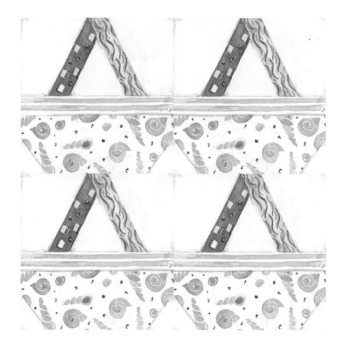

RESURRECTION BUTTERFLY

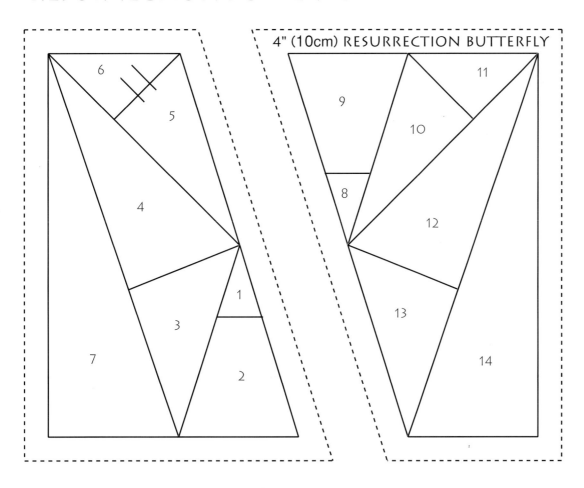

4" (10cm) RESURRECTION BUTTERFLY

PREJOIN THE FABRICS FOR PIECES 5 AND 6; ALIGN THE SEAM, JOINING THESE FABRICS WITH THE SEAM LINE BETWEEN 5 AND 6, THEN SEW THE ENTIRE SEAM JOINING 5/6 TO PIECE 4.

Creative option

LOVE BIRD

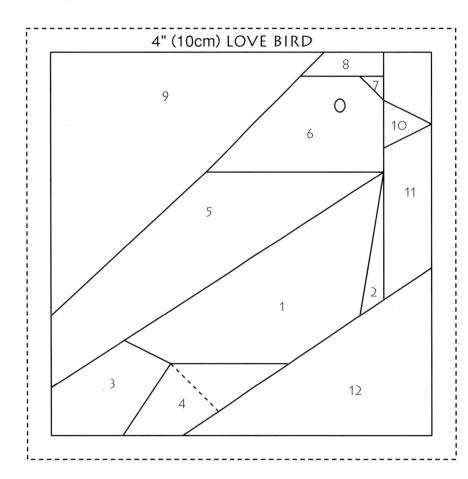

4" (10cm) LOVE BIRD

EYE CAN BE BUTTON OR EMBROIDERY. BEAK SHOULD BE ADDED AS SEPARATE FOLDED 1" (2.5CM) SQUARE (SEWN INTO SEAM WITH PIECE 11). DOTTED LINE SHOWS FOLD LINE FOR PIECE 4 AFTER SEWING.

NOTE: TO SEW PIECE 4, SEE PAGE 19 FOR "STITCH AND TUCK TRICK."

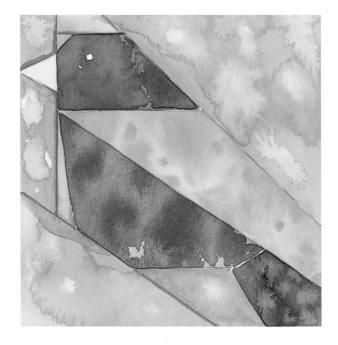

Creative options

SCOTTIE DOG

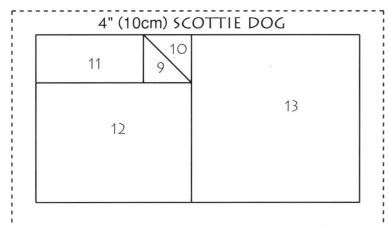

4" (10cm) SCOTTIE DOG

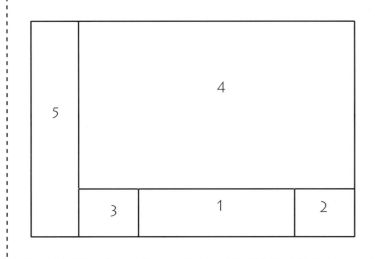

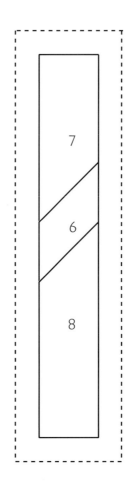

Creative option

PLAYFUL KITTY

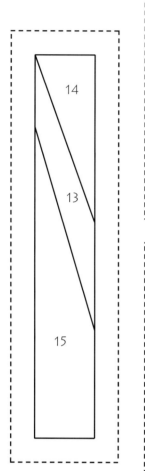

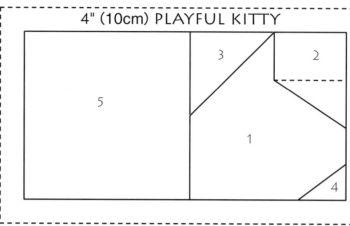

4" (10cm) PLAYFUL KITTY

5   3   2   1   4

14   13   15

NOTE: TO SEW PIECE 4, SEE PAGE 19 FOR "STITCH AND TUCK TRICK."

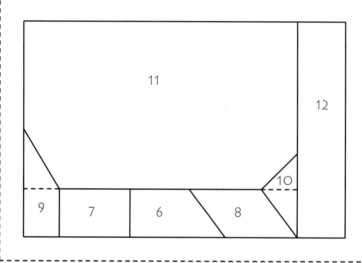

11   12   9   7   6   8   10

Creative option

ROSE IN BLOOM

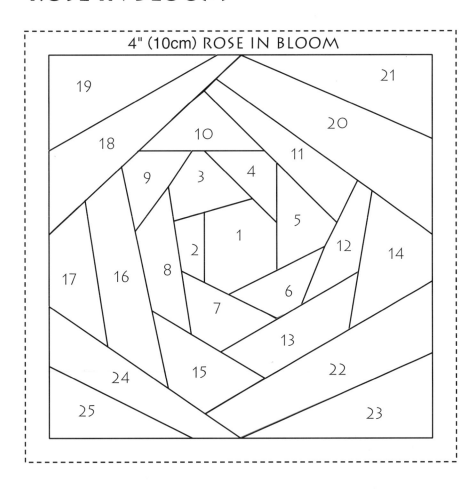

4" (10cm) ROSE IN BLOOM

Creative option

FUCHSIA

Creative options

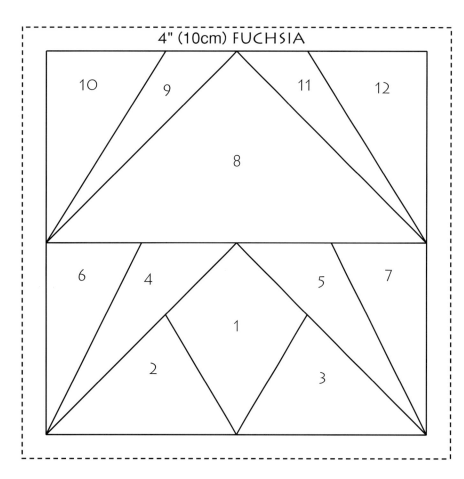

4" (10cm) FUCHSIA

10   9   11   12

8

6   4   5   7

1

2   3

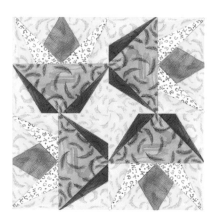

FANTASY VINE

FANTASY VINE

1
2
3
4
5
6
7
8

2½" X 3" (6.5 X 7.5cm)

Creative options

BUD AND BUTTERFLY

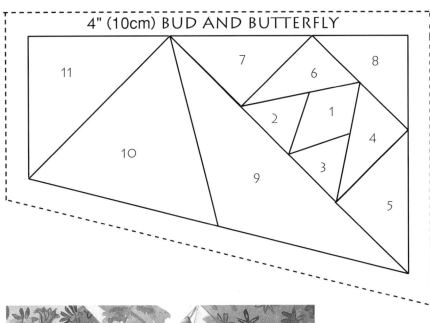

4" (10cm) BUD AND BUTTERFLY

Creative options

HIDDEN FLOWER

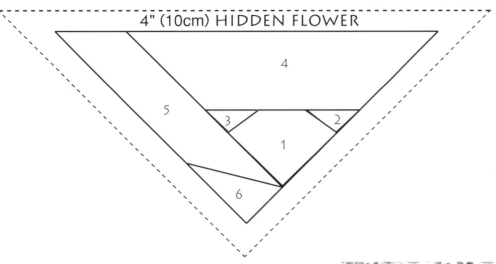

4" (10cm) HIDDEN FLOWER

Creative options

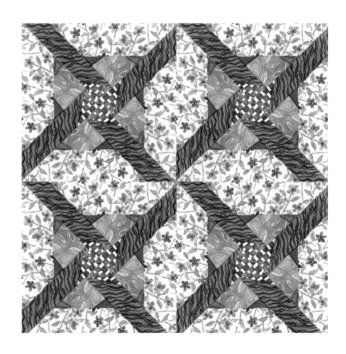

BUTTERFLY III

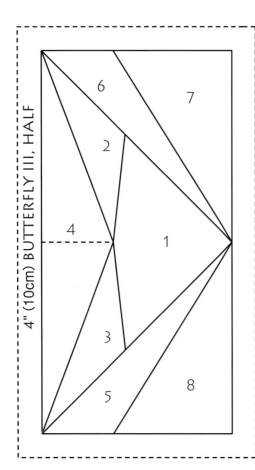
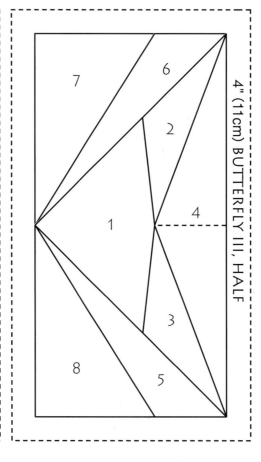

4" (10cm) BUTTERFLY III, HALF

4" (11cm) BUTTERFLY III, HALF

6 7 2 4 1 3 5 8

7 6 2 4 1 3 8 5

INSERT A PIECE OF BLACK PIPING BETWEEN SEAMS FOR BODY. (OPTIONAL) NOTE: TO SEW PIECE 4, SEE PAGE 19 FOR "STITCH AND TUCK TRICK."

Creative option

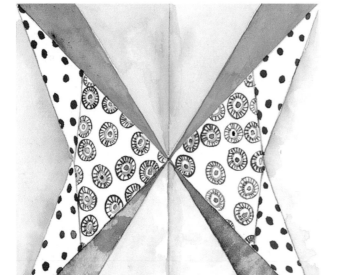

ORIENTAL TULIP

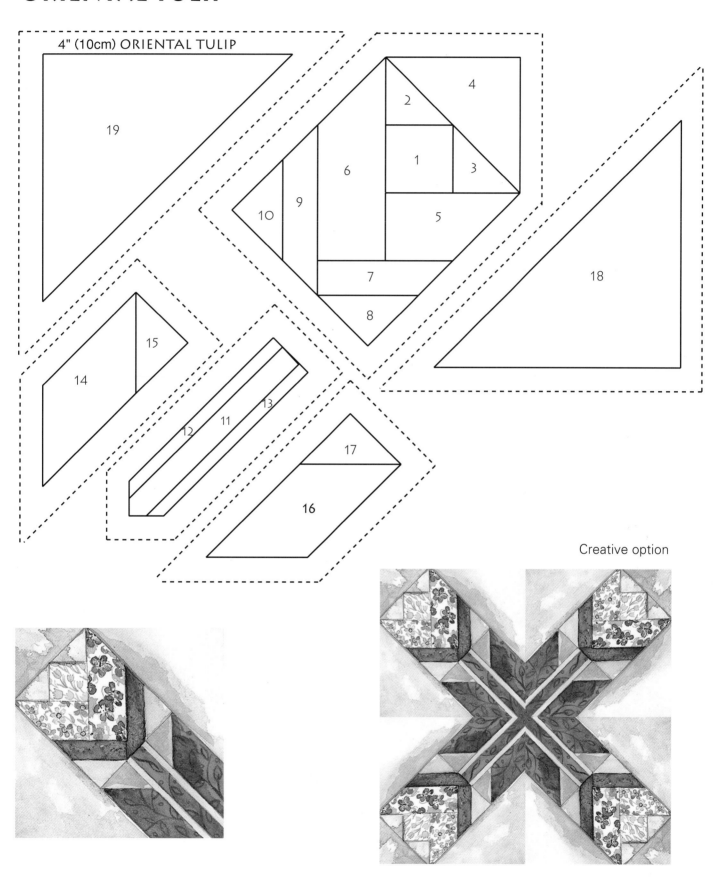

4" (10cm) ORIENTAL TULIP

Creative option

BROMELIAD FLOWER

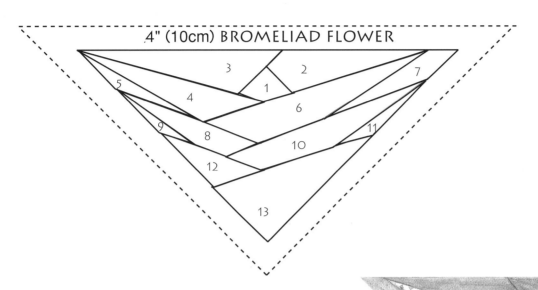

4" (10cm) BROMELIAD FLOWER

Creative options

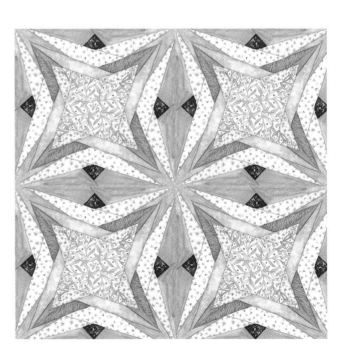

BASKET OF FLOWERS

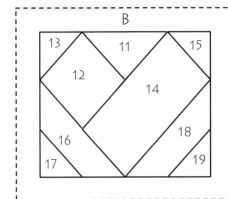

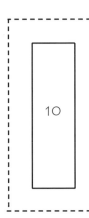

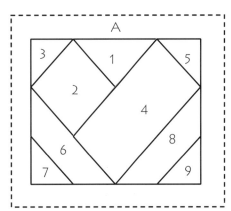

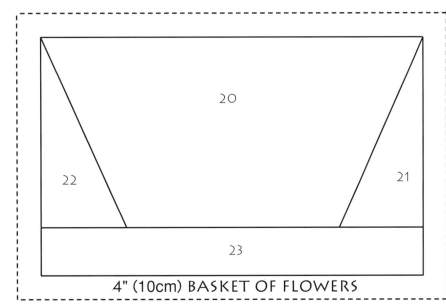

4" (10cm) BASKET OF FLOWERS

Creative option

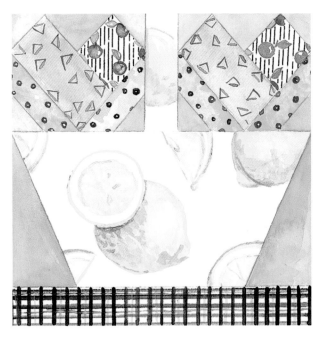

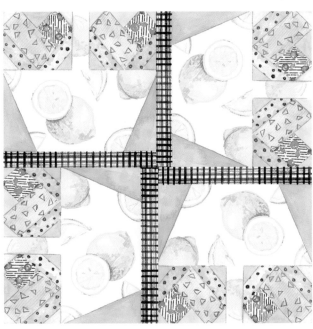

HANDS OF LOVE

The touch of a hand in friendship and affection speaks as loudly as words to the heart. Weave these patterns into your fabric messages.

TESSELLATING HANDS ◆ ◆

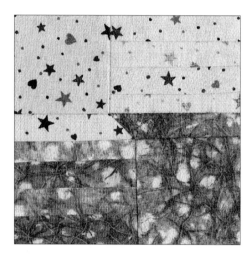

Repeat this pattern over and over to make a wonderful quilt design. Consider using many colors for the hands to express teamwork and community.

HEART IN HAND ◆ ◆ ◆

This block serves well as an explicit Valentine offering your heart to the one you love.

DIAGONAL HEART IN HAND ◆ ◆ ◆

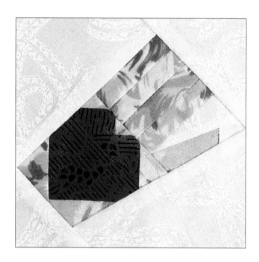

Use this pattern for a corner setting in a heart quilt for your loved one.

HANDS OF FRIENDSHIP ◆ ◆ ◆

Extend a hand in friendship or an offer of love with this block pattern.

TESSELLATING HANDS

4" (10cm) TESSELLATING HANDS

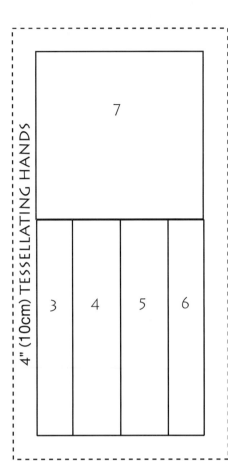
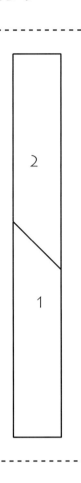
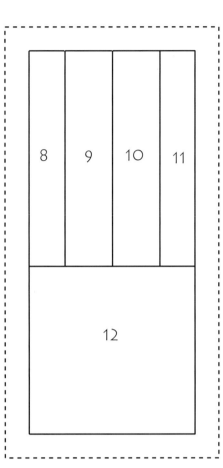

Creative option

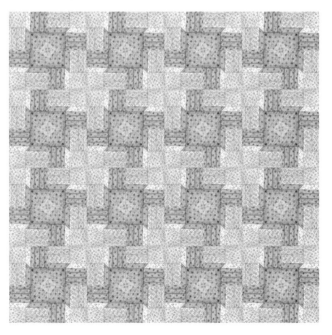

HEART IN HAND

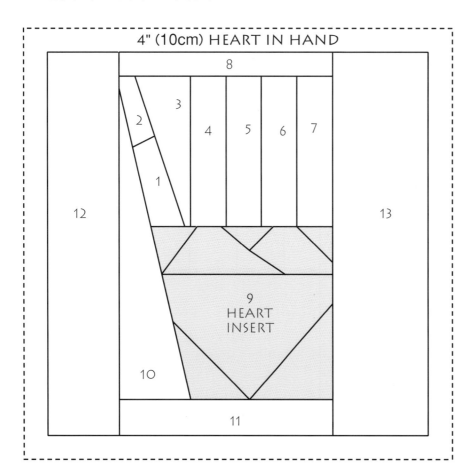

4" (10cm) HEART IN HAND

8
3
2
4 5 6 7
1
12
13
9 HEART INSERT
10
11

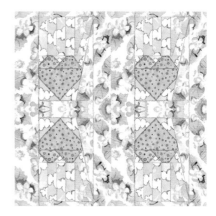

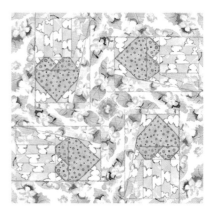

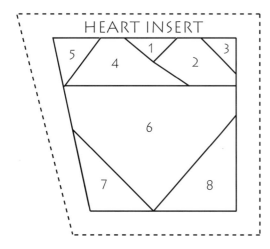

HEART INSERT

5
4 1 2 3
6
7 8

DIAGONAL HEART IN HAND

Creative options

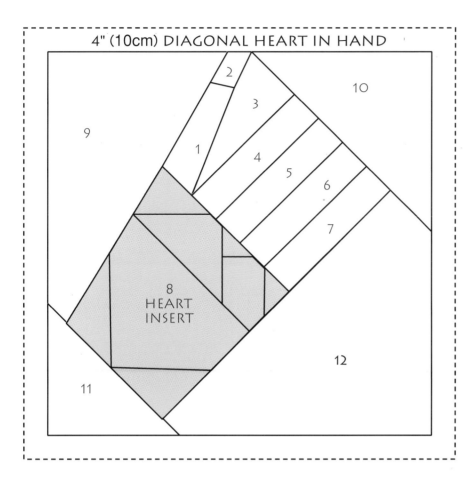

4" (10cm) DIAGONAL HEART IN HAND

2
3
10
9
1
4
5
6
7
8
HEART
INSERT
11
12

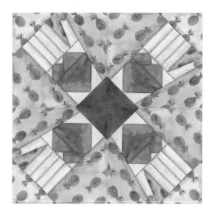

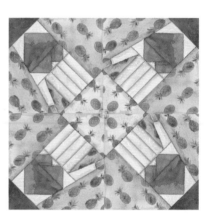

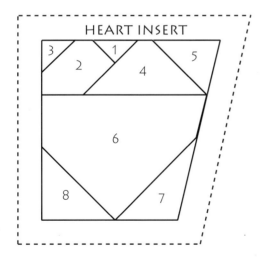

HEART INSERT

3
2
1
4
5
6
8
7

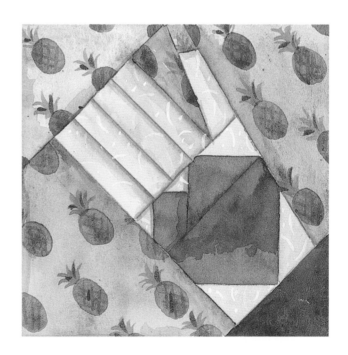

HANDS OF FRIENDSHIP

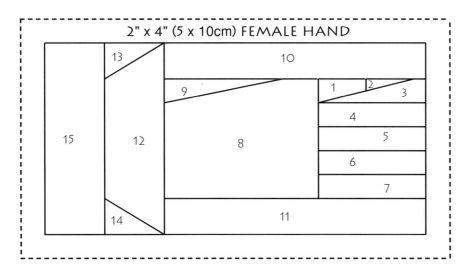

2" x 4" (5 x 10cm) FEMALE HAND

13
10
9
1 2
3
15
12
8
4
5
6
7
14
11

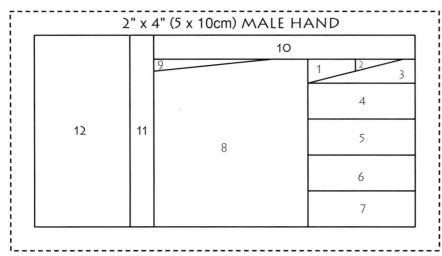

2" x 4" (5 x 10cm) MALE HAND

10
9
1 2
3
12
11
8
4
5
6
7

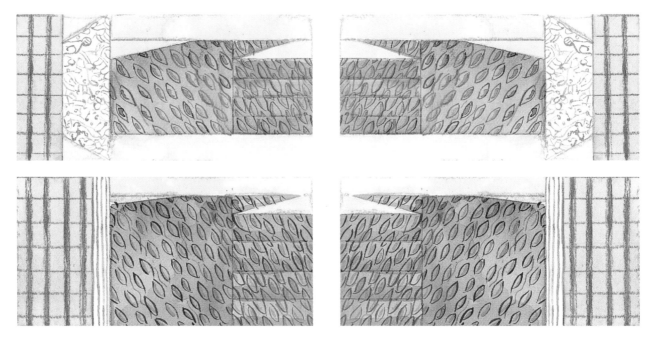

TEA PARTIES AND PICNICS

What's more romantic than an afternoon outing? Whether it's a fancy tea party or a breezy summer picnic, these blocks will help you make a fabric occasion to cherish.

ICE CREAM CONE ♦

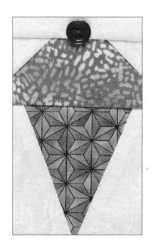

Ice cream is a sweet treat to share with friends or lovers, and this delicious block will surely add a nice touch to a special friendship quilt.

ICE CREAM SUNDAE ♦

Share a sundae with a special friend, or make a whole quilt full of flavors for that calorie-free treat.

TEA PARTY DELIGHTS ♦

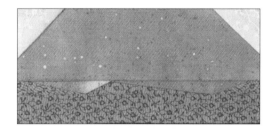

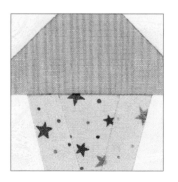

Cupcakes and tea cake make special party fare. Enjoy them in your favorite fabric tea party.

PICNIC BASKET ◆

Pack up this basket and add some treats to remember a favorite outing or start a new tradition.

FRIENDSHIP MUG ◆ ◆

Make a whole cupboard full of special mugs for your kitchen.

FRIENDSHIP MUG WITH HEART ◆ ◆

The design of this mug expresses your feelings for good friends or Valentines.

CUP AND SAUCER ◆ ◆

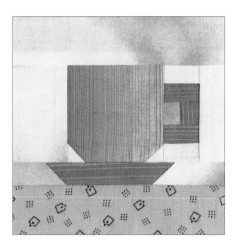

Clinking porcelain sounds so sweet when accompanied by a friend's laughter. Have fun choosing wild prints for a fancy collection of these charming sets.

COFFEE POT ◆ ◆ ◆

Remember that special coffee pot Grandma used when you were a child? Recapture that warm memory with this block.

TEAPOT ◆ ◆ ◆

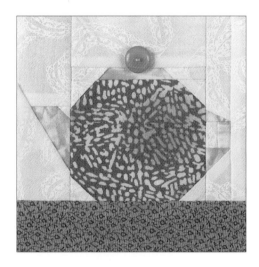

What could be more pleasant than spending an afternoon over a warm pot of steaming tea—call in your friends and enjoy!

ICE CREAM CONE

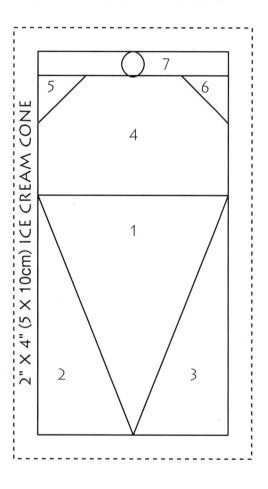

USE 1/4" (6MM) OR 3/8" (1CM) BUTTON FOR CHERRY.

ICE CREAM SUNDAE

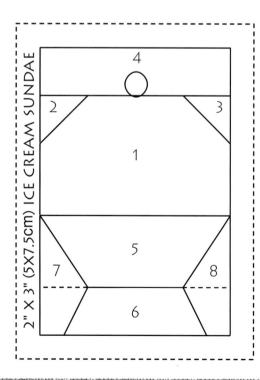

CHERRY CAN BE A 1/4" (6MM) OR 3/8" (1CM) BUTTON; DASHED INTERNAL LINES DENOTE FOLD/TUCK IN FABRIC OF PIECES 7 AND 8.

NOTE: TO SEW PIECES 7 AND 8, SEE PAGE 19 FOR "STITCH AND TUCK TRICK."

TEA PARTY DELIGHTS

2" X 4" (5X10cm) CUPCAKE

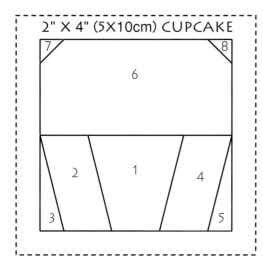

2" X 4" (5 X 10cm) TEA CAKE

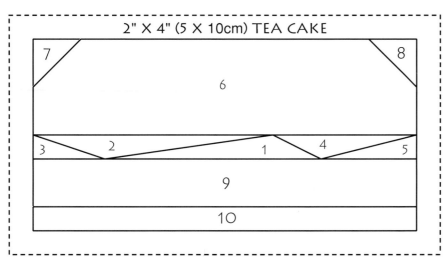

PICNIC BASKET

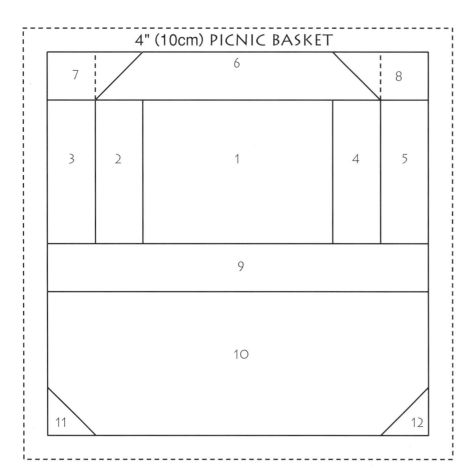

4" (10cm) PICNIC BASKET

DOTTED LINES SHOW FOLD LINE FOR PIECES 7 AND 8, AFTER SEWING.

NOTE: TO SEW PIECES 7 AND 8, SEE PAGE 19 FOR "STITCH AND TUCK TRICK."

Creative options

FRIENDSHIP MUG

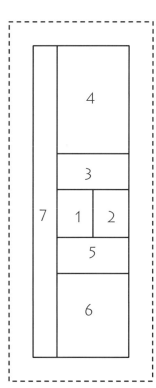

4" (10cm) FRIENDSHIP MUG

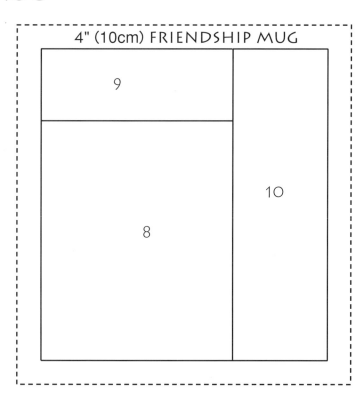

9

10

8

11

Creative option

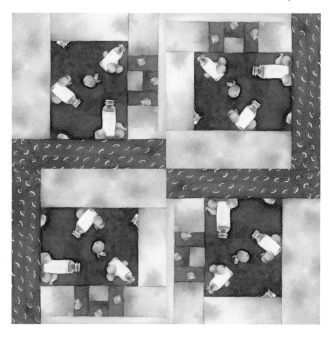

FRIENDSHIP MUG WITH HEART

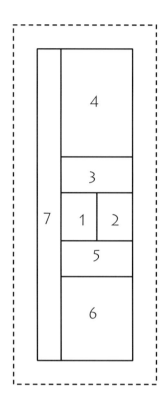

4

3

7 | 1 | 2

5

6

4" (10cm) FRIENDSHIP MUG WITH HEART

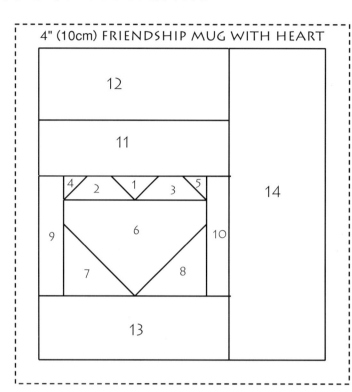

12

11

4 | 2 | 1 | 3 | 5

14

9 | 6 | 10

7 | 8

13

11

Creative option

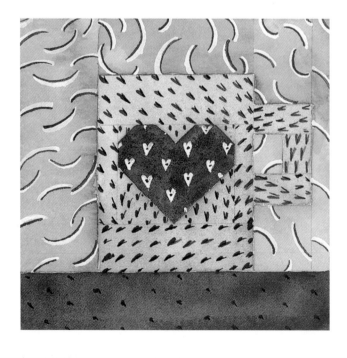

CUP AND SAUCER

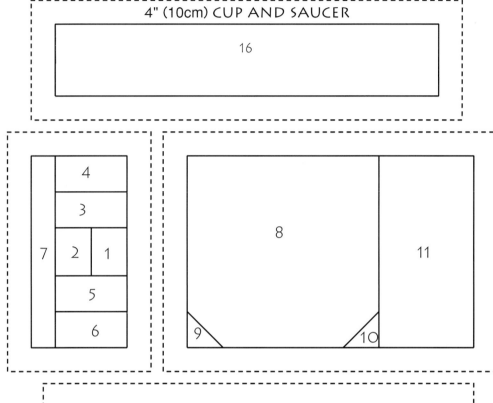

4" (10cm) CUP AND SAUCER

16

| 4 |
| 3 |
| 7 | 2 | 1 |
| 5 |
| 6 |

8   11

9   10

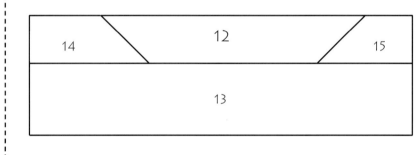

14   12   15

13

Creative option

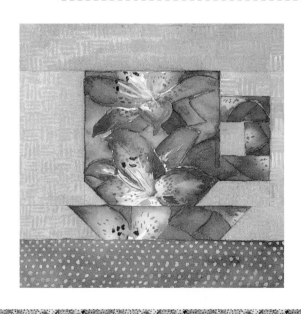

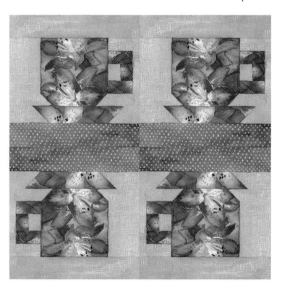

TEAPOT

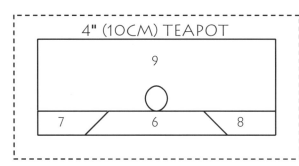

4" (10CM) TEAPOT

9

7 6 8

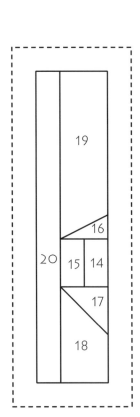

19
16
20 15 14
17
18

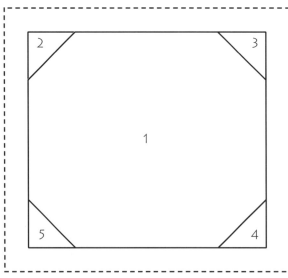

2 3
1
5 4

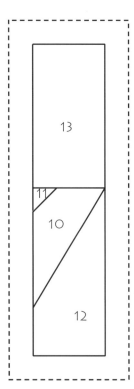

13
11
10
12

21

Creative option

CHOOSE A 1/4"
(6MM) OR 3/8"
(1CM) BUTTON
FOR TEAPOT
TOPPER. YOU
MAY CHOOSE
TO COVER
YOUR BUTTON
IN A FABRIC
THAT MATCHES
YOUR TEAPOT.

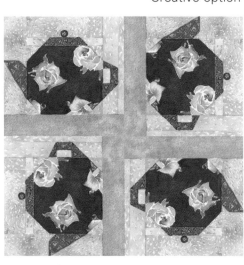

COFFEE POT

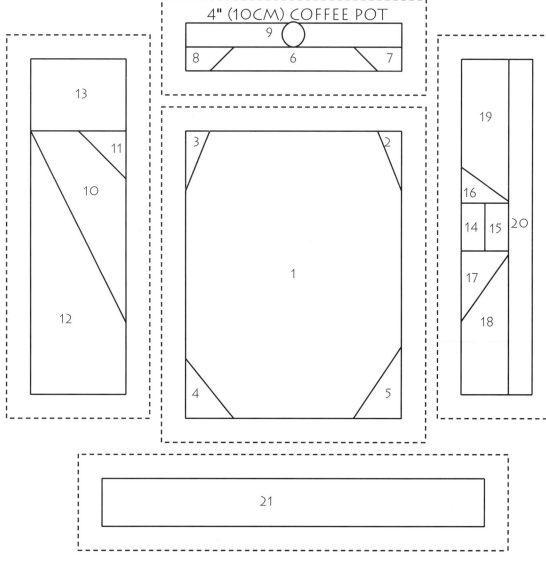

4" (10CM) COFFEE POT

9

8   6   7

13

11

10

12

3   2

1

4   5

19

16

14 15 20

17

18

21

CHOOSE A
1/4" (6MM)
OR 3/8" (1CM)
BUTTON
FOR COFFEE
POT TOPPER.
YOU MAY
CHOOSE TO
COVER YOUR
BUTTON IN
A FABRIC
THAT
MATCHES
YOUR
COFFEE POT.

Creative option

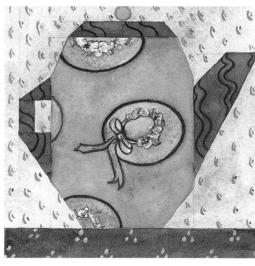

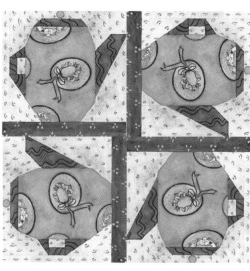

SPECIAL VALENTINES

These blocks are inspired by one of the most magical experiences—being in love. Share these with the special person in your life.

CUPID'S ARROW ◆

(INSERTION PATTERN)

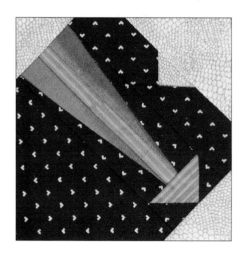

The quick dart of love strikes many an unsuspecting person. Send your loving wishes with this Valentine insert block.

FALLING IN LOVE ◆ ◆ ◆

Capture all the excitement of that dizzying experience of being in love with this block.

LOVE ◆ ◆ ◆

(INSERTION PATTERN)

You can clearly spell out your feelings for your most special Valentine with this block.

SWEET NOTHINGS ◆◆

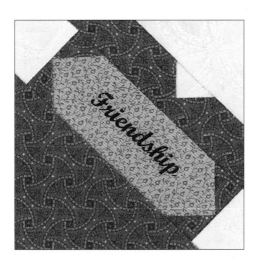

Remember those candy hearts with Valentine messages we ate as children? Make your own here. Rubber-stamp or letter your thoughts to a friend or loved one right onto this block and re-create that childhood fun!

LOVE AT HOME ◆◆◆

(INSERTION PATTERN)

This house is brimming with love, capturing the feeling of love at home. Make one for your next quilt.

WRAPPED IN LOVE ◆◆◆

(INSERTION PATTERN)

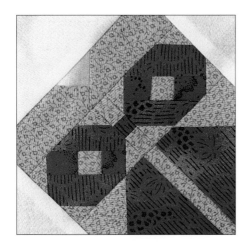

Wrap up your love with a special bow using this pattern.

CUPID'S ARROW

(INSERTION PATTERN)

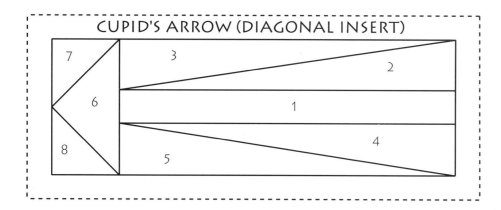

CUPID'S ARROW (DIAGONAL INSERT)

Creative options

FALLING IN LOVE

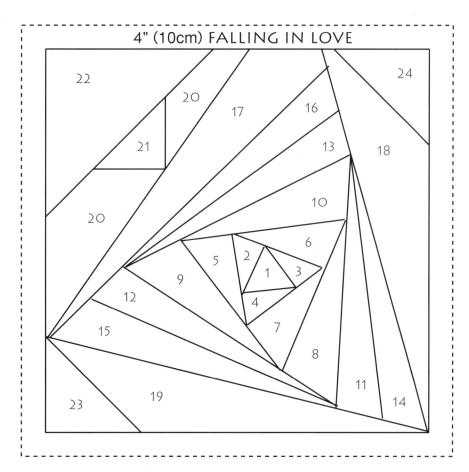

4" (10cm) FALLING IN LOVE

SEW THE TWO 20 PIECES AS ONE STRIP. AFTER SEWING PIECE 21, FOLD ALONG DOTTED LINE TO PRESS UPWARD.

NOTE: TO SEW PIECE 21, SEE PAGE 19 FOR "STITCH AND TUCK TRICK."

Creative options

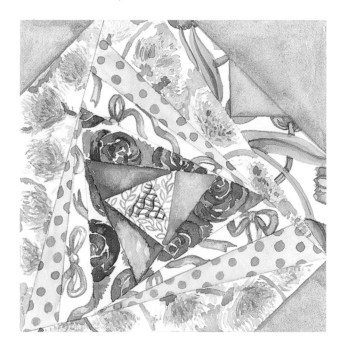

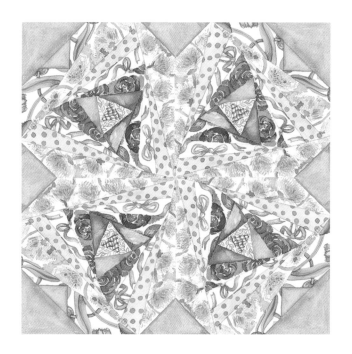

LOVE
(INSERTION PATTERN)

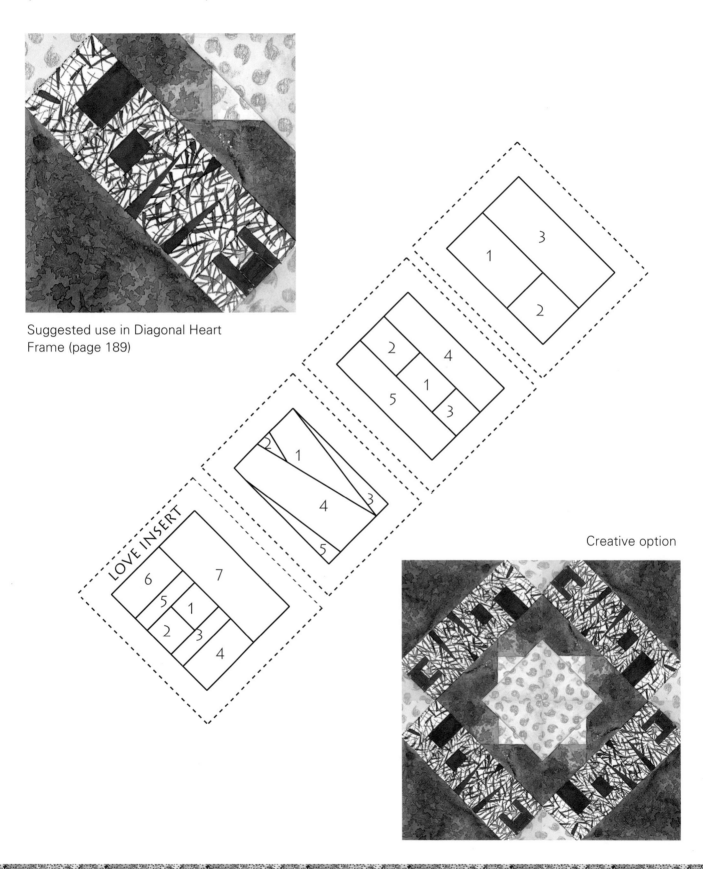

Suggested use in Diagonal Heart
Frame (page 189)

Creative option

SWEET NOTHINGS

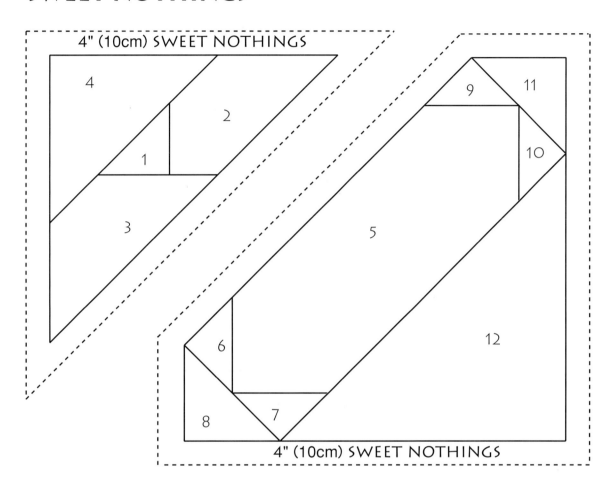

4" (10cm) SWEET NOTHINGS

4" (10cm) SWEET NOTHINGS

Creative option

WRAPPED IN LOVE

(INSERTION PATTERN)

FOR USE WITH DIAGONAL HEART FRAME PATTERN ON PAGE 184. USE MODIFIED PIECE BELOW.

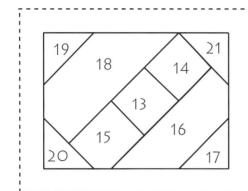

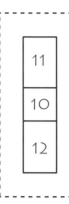

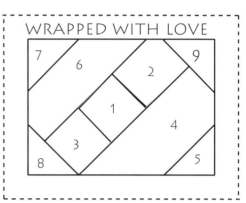
WRAPPED WITH LOVE

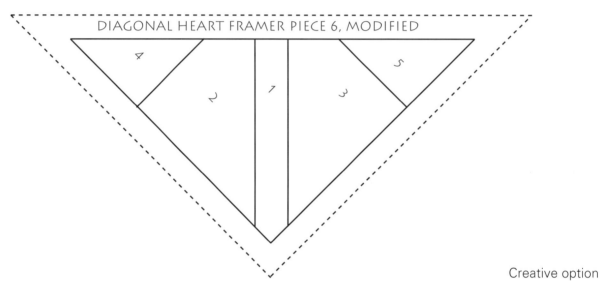
DIAGONAL HEART FRAMER PIECE 6, MODIFIED

Creative option

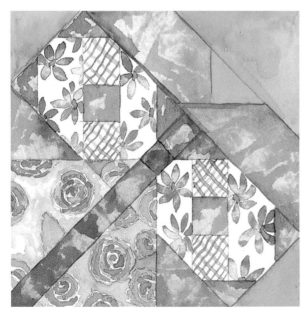

LOVE AT HOME

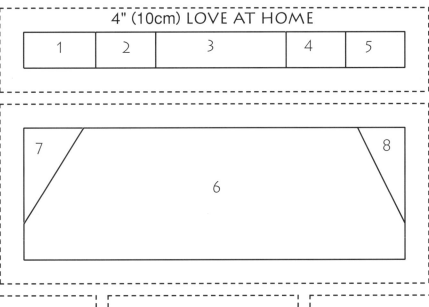

4" (10cm) LOVE AT HOME

| 1 | 2 | 3 | 4 | 5 |

7   6   8

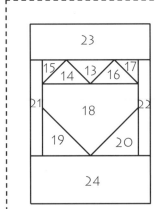

23
15 14 13 16 17
21   18   22
19   20
24

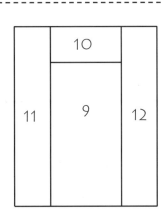

10
11   9   12

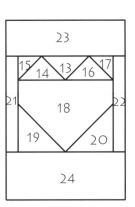

23
15 14 13 16 17
21   18   22
19   20
24

25

Creative option

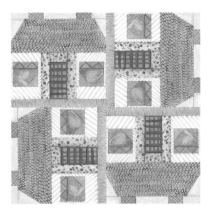

BORDERS

Here are border patterns that will add
the perfect finish to your quilts. Don't
overlook using them as quilt medallions.

BRICK BORDER

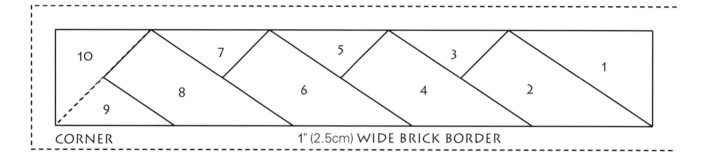

TWISTED RIBBON BORDER

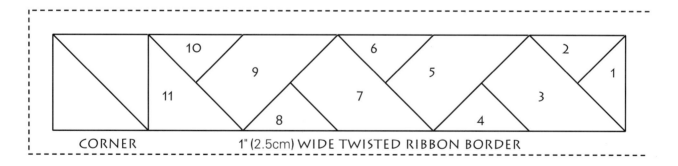

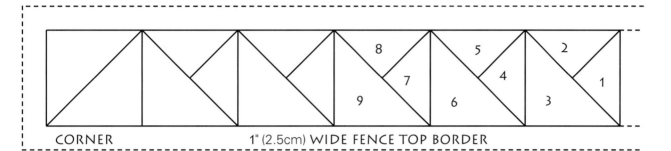

FENCE TOP BORDER

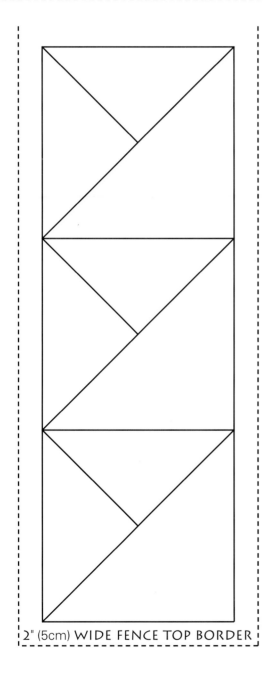

CORNER   1" (2.5cm) WIDE FENCE TOP BORDER

2" (5cm) WIDE FENCE TOP BORDER

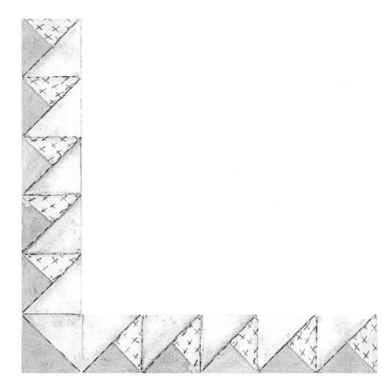

LATTICE FENCE BORDER

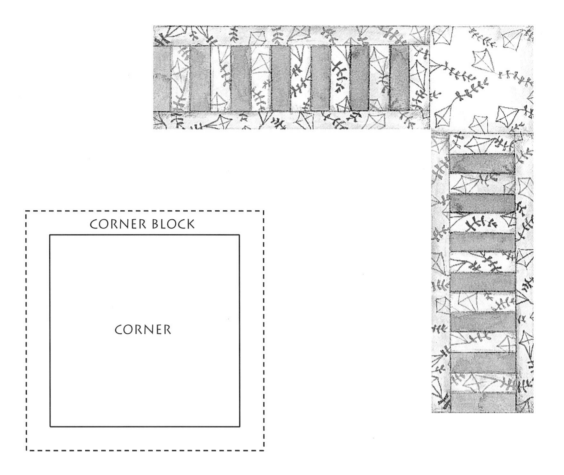

```
┌─────────────────────────────────┐
│         CORNER BLOCK            │
│   ┌─────────────────────────┐   │
│   │                         │   │
│   │                         │   │
│   │                         │   │
│   │        CORNER           │   │
│   │                         │   │
│   │                         │   │
│   │                         │   │
│   └─────────────────────────┘   │
└─────────────────────────────────┘
```

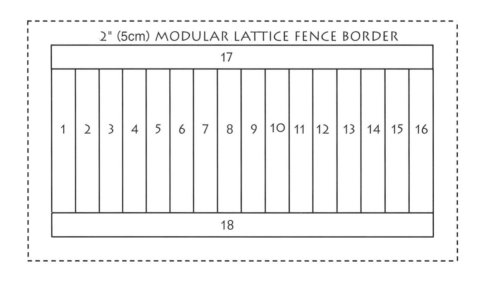

2" (5cm) MODULAR LATTICE FENCE BORDER

17
1 2 3 4 5 6 7 8 9 10 11 12 13 14 15 16
18

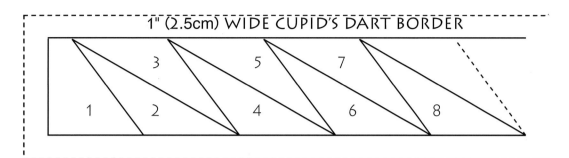

CUPID'S DART BORDER

1" (2.5cm) WIDE CUPID'S DART BORDER

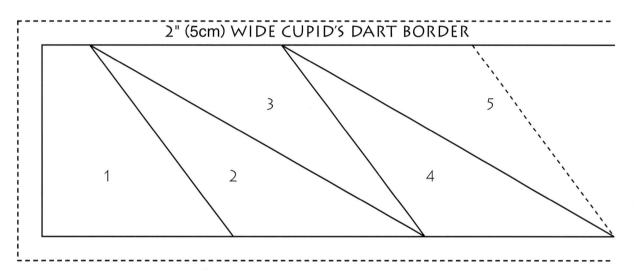

1   3   2   5   4   7   6   8

2" (5cm) WIDE CUPID'S DART BORDER

1   3   2   5   4

Creative options

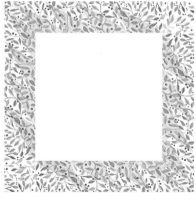

STRING OF HEARTS BORDER

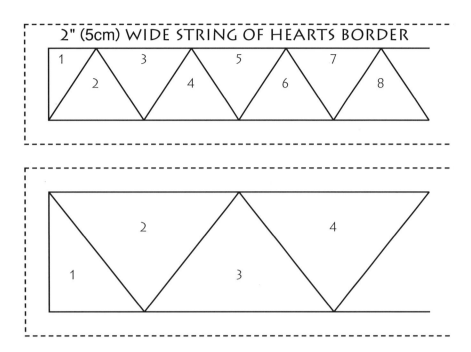

2" (5cm) WIDE STRING OF HEARTS BORDER

1   2   3   4   5   6   7   8

1   2   3   4

Creative option

TINY HEARTS BORDER

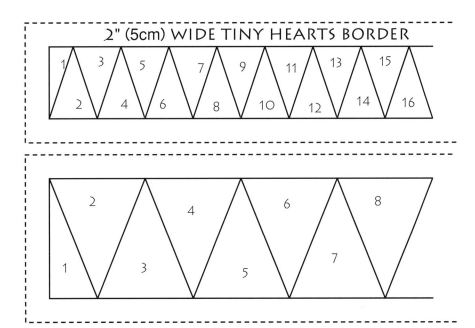

2" (5cm) WIDE TINY HEARTS BORDER

| 1 | 3 | 5 | 7 | 9 | 11 | 13 | 15 |
| 2 | 4 | 6 | 8 | 10 | 12 | 14 | 16 |

| 2 | 4 | 6 | 8 |
| 1 | 3 | 5 | 7 |

Creative options

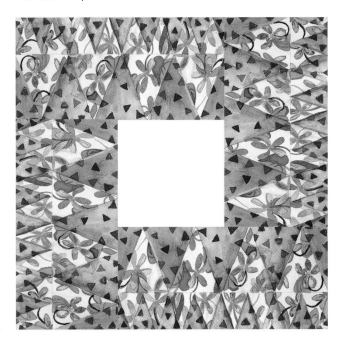

TESSELLATING STRING OF HEARTS BORDER

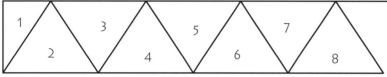

2¾" (7cm) WIDE TESSELLATING STRING OF HEARTS BORDER

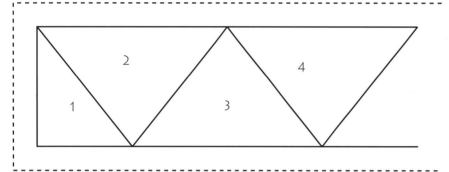

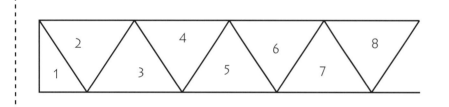

Creative options

TESSELLATING TINY HEARTS BORDER

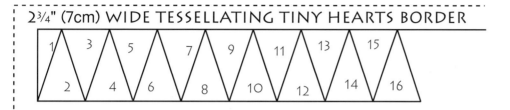

2¾" (7cm) WIDE TESSELLATING TINY HEARTS BORDER

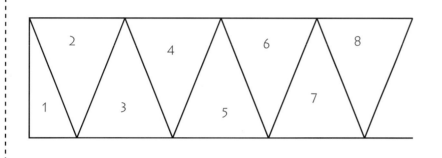

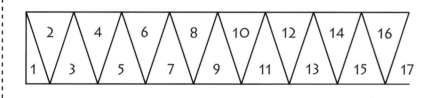

Creative options

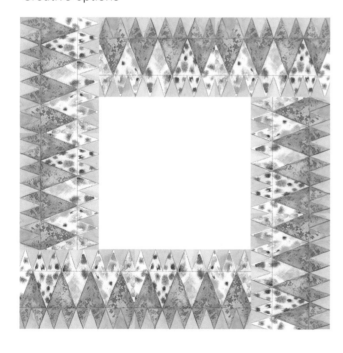

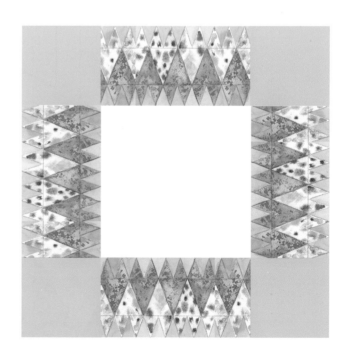

EQUILATERAL TRIANGULAR BORDER

FRAME BORDERS

HALF SQUARE TRIANGULAR BORDER

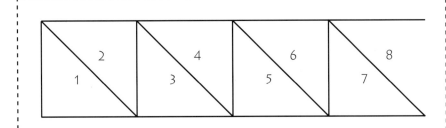

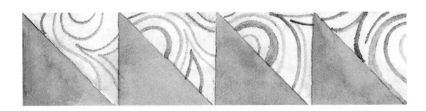

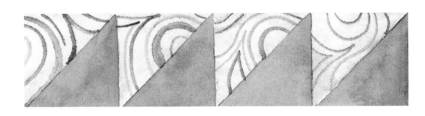

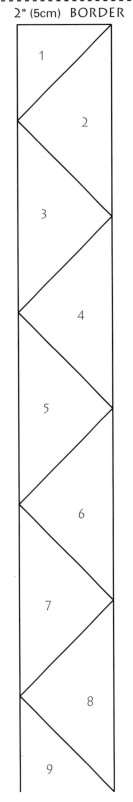

2" (5cm) BORDER

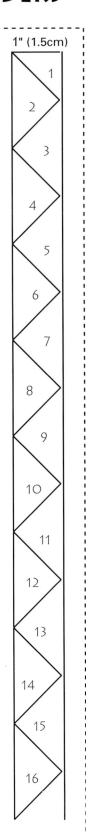

1" (1.5cm)

◆ PART THREE ◆

FINISHING

FINISHING

This chapter contains instructions for completing your quilt top, making the quilt "sandwich," binding your quilt, and adding a sleeve for hanging. Refer to the general quilting titles listed in the bibliography for thorough discussions of these topics as well as for excellent books on machine quilting.

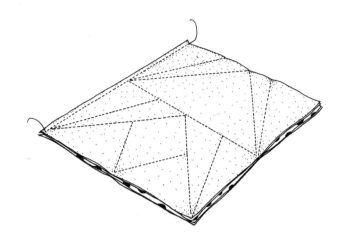

JOINING THE BLOCKS

Lay out the blocks according to the layout diagram for the quilt you are making. Beginning at the top left corner, match the adjoining sides of the first two blocks together, right sides facing. Since pins tend to distort the paper foundations, use a paper clip to hold the match points in place. Baste ¼" (6mm) from the raw edge, as marked on the foundation. Check to make sure seams match and points meet where necessary. Stitch.

Vinyl-coated paper clips are especially good to use as the vinyl protects your fabric from marks that uncoated metal paper clips may leave.

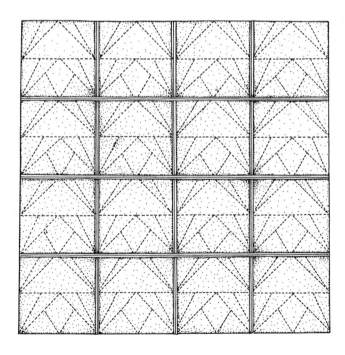

Keep adding blocks until you have completed the top horizontal row. Do the same for each remaining row. Press seam allowances open. Stitch the rows together, carefully matching seams. Press seam allowances open.

NOTE: Some block patterns include strategic points that must match when the rows are stitched. In this case I baste the blocks together, check the alignment, and then stitch when I'm satisfied they match up properly.

REMOVING THE PAPER

If you used paper as the foundation for your quilt, gently tear the paper from the backs of the blocks now, as if you were tearing stamps. Press the blocks gently, lifting the iron up and down rather than dragging it, so as not to distort the blocks.

For easier paper removal, after stitching a seam, score the paper at the seam while trimming. When you're ready to remove the paper, dampen it slightly with a sponge or spray it once with a fine spray. Don't get it too wet. If you do, just press it a bit with a warm iron.
—Annie Toth, Moorpark, CA

You may wish to measure the finished block to be sure it is an accurate square and not distorted, though this is not usually necessary. On the rare occasion the block is distorted, "block" it by dampening it and then pinning it to a marked square of the correct size. Allow to dry. Press.

For easy paper removal, photocopy on a cheap-grade typing paper or onion skin paper, then press the finished block to scorch the paper. The paper becomes brittle and you can practically "snap" it off!
—Annie Toth, Moorpark, CA

BASTING AND QUILTING

Now your quilt top is ready to be made into a quilt.

1. Cut the backing and batting about 1" (2.5cm) larger all around than the quilt top.

2. Lay the backing wrong side up on a large, flat surface.

3. Lay the batting on top.

4. Lay the quilt, right side up, on top of the backing and batting.

5. Working from the center out, thread or safety-pin baste the three layers of the quilt "sandwich" together.

6. Quilt as desired.

7. Remove all basting stitches or remaining safety pins.

BINDING

You may bind your quilt—finish the outer edge with fabric—by either folding the backing to the front and stitching in place, or adding a separate strip of fabric.

NOTE: While they are a perfectly acceptable finish for a wall quilt, self-bindings may not be the best choice for a bed quilt. For these, use an attached binding strip. The double fabric of this type of binding will better withstand the wear and tear of everyday use.

SELF-BINDING

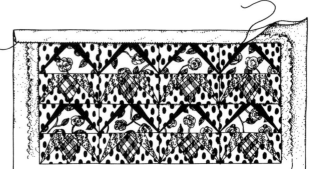

1. Trim the batting even with the quilt top. Trim the backing to ¾" (2cm) larger than the outer edge of the quilt all around.

2. Along one edge, fold the backing ¼" (6mm) to the front. Fold the backing to the front, over the edges of the batting and quilt top. Fold the sides in first, and slipstitch by hand or topstitch by machine. Repeat at top and bottom.

ATTACHED BINDING

1. Trim the batting and backing to be even with the quilt top.

2. To determine how long a binding to make, add the measurements of the four sides of your quilt top and an extra 8" (20cm).

3. Cut strips of binding along the straight, crosswise grain (there is some give to the crosswise grain) of your fabric. Use a diagonal seam to piece the strips together if necessary.

For a quilt show–quality finish, join the ends of the binding one-third away from the bottom right-hand edge of the quilt. This is the least noticeable join location and is the choice of award-winning quilters.

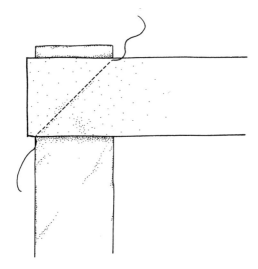

NOTE: The width of your binding strips is determined by the size of your quilt. For a wall hanging–size quilt, the finished binding that shows on the front surface should be about ¼" (6mm). The larger size of a bed quilt requires a finished binding of ½" (1.5cm) or wider for proper proportion. As an easy rule of thumb, cut your binding strips 1¾" (4.5cm) wide for wall hangings and 3¼" (8cm) wide for bed quilts.

4. Wrong sides together, fold the seamed strips in half lengthwise. Press.

5. From right side and matching raw edges, place the binding strip along one edge of the quilt top. Machine stitch the binding to the quilt "sandwich," using a ¼" (6mm) seam allowance, depending on the desired finished binding width. Leave the first 3" (7.5cm) or so of the binding loose so that you can join the two ends of the binding later.

6. At the first corner, stop stitching ¼" (6mm) from the edge of the quilt top. Raise the presser foot, but leave the needle down, in the fabric.

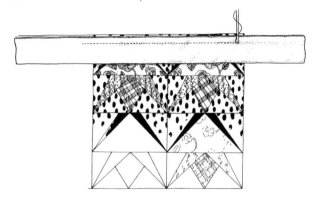

Pivot, and stitch diagonally to the corner of the quilt and off.

Hold the binding so the loose edge is straight up from the next side.

Fold the loose binding edge down, matching the raw edge to that of the next side of the quilt, and sew to the next corner.

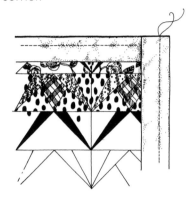

Repeat for the remaining corners.

7. When you approach about 4" (10cm) of the beginning of the binding, stop stitching. Match the ends of the binding as shown, opening them up to stitch them together along the diagonal. Refold and finish sewing the seam.

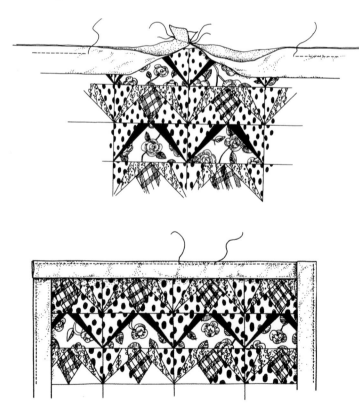

8. Fold the binding to the back of the quilt over the raw edges of the quilt "sandwich," covering the machine stitching at the back of the quilt. Slipstitch the binding in place.

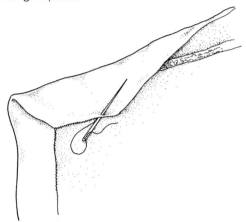

"Love is, above all, the gift of oneself."
—Jean Anouith
Ardele

ADDING A SLEEVE FOR HANGING

To hang a small quilt on a wall, sew a simple sleeve to the back. A rod or ⅜"–¾" (1–2cm) dowel slipped into the sleeve provides the support to hang your quilt nicely. Cut the dowel 1" (2.5cm) longer than the sleeve.

1. Cut a strip of fabric 3½" (8.5cm) wide and as long as the width of your quilt less 1" (2.5cm) to 2" (5cm).

Press each short edge ¼" (6mm) to the wrong side twice. Topstitch.

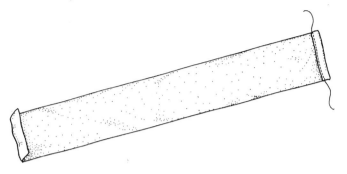

2. Wrong sides together, fold the sleeve strip lengthwise in half. Center the raw edge of the strip along the top edge of the back of the quilt before attaching the binding. Baste.

3. Stitch the binding to the quilt as instructed above, securing the sleeve in the seam.

4. Slipstitch the bottom, folded edge of the sleeve to the back of the quilt.

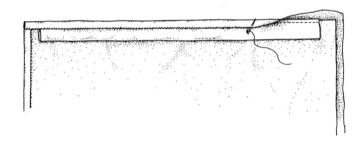

"I've memorized your face and the way you look at me... it melts my heart every time I think about it."
—Renée Duvall

◆ PART FOUR ◆

QUILT DESIGNS

COUNTRY COUSINS QUILT

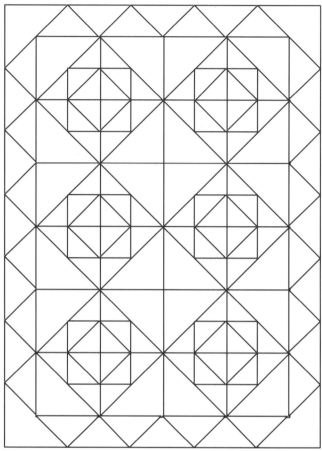

FINISHED SIZE: 10" × 14" (25.5 × 35.5cm)

FABRIC REQUIREMENTS: 1¼ yard (114.5cm) each
  of two fabrics

BLOCKS: Two 3" (7.5cm) wide and four 2" (5cm)
  wide strips 40" (101.5cm) long for each of
  two colors

BORDER: Two 3" (7.5cm) wide strips of each for
  two colors

BACKING: 12" × 16" (30.5 × 40.5cm)

BATTING: 12" × 16" (30.5 × 40.5cm)

♦ **COUNTRY COUSINS (page 44)**

  2" (5cm) block size

  Make 24

♦ **FRAME BORDER (page 247)**

  1" (2.5cm) wide

Make 2 to finish 8" (20.5cm) for top and
  bottom borders

Make 2 to finish 14" (35.5cm) for side borders
  (includes corner pieces)

  This design is most effective when it is done
in two colors, such as blue and white, and makes
a wonderful scrap quilt: choose scraps within
two color choices. Fabric requirements are for a
two-color (two-fabric) quilt.

CRAZY QUILT

FINISHED SIZE: 14" × 18" (35.5 × 45.5cm)

FABRIC REQUIREMENTS:

BLOCKS: Scraps of many fabrics

BORDER: Scraps at least 1½" (4cm) wide

BACKING: 16" × 20" (40.5 × 51cm)

BATTING: 16" × 20" (40.5 × 51cm)

♦ **CRAZY PATCH I (page 26)**

    4" (10cm) block size

    Make 3

♦ **CRAZY PATCH II (page 26)**

    4" (10cm) block size

    Make 3

♦ **CRAZY PATCH III (page 27)**

    4" (10cm) block size

    Make 3

♦ **CRAZY PATCH IV (page 27)**

    4" (10cm) block size

    Make 3

♦ **EQUILATERAL TRIANGLE BORDER (page 246)**

    1" (2.5cm) wide

Make 2 to finish 12" (30cm) on the short side and 13" (33cm) on the long (out) side for the top and bottom borders

Make 2 to finish 16" (40.5cm) on the short side and 18" (45.5cm) on the long side (includes corner triangles) for side borders

Crazy Quilt offers an opportunity to use scraps of velveteen, lamé, and other noncotton fabrics. Use a permanent foundation to give the fabrics stability.

DELECTABLE MOUNTAINS QUILT

FINISHED SIZE: 20" × 20" (51 × 51cm)

FABRIC REQUIREMENTS: 1¼ yard (114.5cm) each
of two fabrics

DELECTABLE MOUNTAINS BLOCKS: Three 4"
(10cm) wide strips 40" (101.5cm) long and
seven 1½" (4cm) wide strips 40" (101.5cm)
long for each of two colors (mountains and
background)

BORDER: Five 3" (7.5cm) wide strips 40" (101.5cm)
long for each of two colors

BACKING: 22" × 22" (56 × 56cm)

BATTING: 22" × 22" (56 × 56cm)

♦ **DELECTABLE MOUNTAINS (page 36)**

4" (10cm) block size

Make 16

♦ **HALF-SQUARE TRIANGULAR BORDER (page 245)**

2" (5cm) wide

Make 2 strips for top and bottom borders with 4 triangles in one orientation and 4 in the other for
a finished total length of 16" (40.5cm) each

Make 2 strips for the side borders with 5 triangles in
one orientation and 5 in the other for a total finished length of 20" (51cm) each (includes corner blocks)

This pattern works best when done in two colors, or as a scrap quilt within these color choices.

GEESE BY THE CABIN QUILT

FINISHED SIZE: 14" × 14" (35.5 × 35.5cm)

FABRIC REQUIREMENTS:

BLOCKS: Scraps 1½" (4cm), 3" (7.5cm), and 5"
(13cm) wide in dark- and light-colored "logs"

One 1½" (4cm) wide strip for the center blocks,
traditionally red or yellow

BORDER: Four strips 3" (7.5cm) wide and
40" (101.5cm) long each of dark colors
and of background

BACKING: 16" × 16" (40.5 × 40.5cm)

BATTING: 16" × 16" (40.5 × 40.5cm)

◆ **CABIN GEESE (page 86)**

4" (10cm) block size

Make 9

◆ **FRAME BORDER (page 247)**

1" (2.5cm) wide

Make 2 to finish 12" (30cm) long for top and
bottom borders

Make 2 to finish 14" (35.5cm) for sides (includes
corner block)

This pattern looks best if the corner "geese"
triangles are all the same color. It makes a wonderful scrap quilt in light and dark fabrics.

INDEPENDENCE DAY QUILT

FINISHED SIZE: 11⅝" × 11⅝" (29.5 × 29.5cm)

FABRIC REQUIREMENTS:

CENTER: 3" × 3" (7.5 × 7.5cm) square of fabric

OLD GLORY BLOCKS: One 2" × 8" (5 × 20.5cm) scrap of blue

One 5" × 12" (13 × 30cm) scrap of red

One 5" × 10" (13 × 25.5cm) scrap of white

ROMAN CANDLE BLOCKS: Two 3" (7.5cm) wide strips 40" (101.5cm) long of blue

Two 5" (13cm) wide strips 40" (101.5cm) long of red

One 5" (7.5cm) wide strip 40" (101.5cm) long of white

Three 3" (7.5cm) wide strips 40" (101.5cm) long of white

OUTER BORDER: Two strips 1" × 12½" (2.5 × 31.5cm) and two strips 1" × 14½" (2.5 × 37cm) of blue

BACKING: 14" × 14" (35.5 × 35.5cm)

BATTING: 14" × 14" (35.5 × 35.5cm)

◆ **ROMAN CANDLE (page 59)**

4" (10cm) block size

Make 4 (sixteen 2" [5cm] subunit block foundations)

◆ **OLD GLORY (page 60)**

4" (10cm) block size

Make 4

Add a personal touch to the center block with a rubber-stamped or stenciled patriotic image or ink signature, or use a figured fabric.

INDIAN TRAILS QUILT

FINISHED SIZE: 18" × 18" (45.5 × 45.5cm)

FABRIC REQUIREMENTS:

BLOCKS: FOR LONGEST STRIP: One piece 6"
(15 cm) wide and 25" (63.5 cm) long

FOR MEDIUM STRIP: One piece 4" (10 cm) wide
and 25" (63.5 cm) long

FOR SHORT STRIP: One piece 2½" (6.5 cm) wide
and 25" (63.5 cm) long

FOR BACKGROUND: Two strips 3½" (9 cm) wide
and 40" (101.5 cm) long

Four strips 2" (5cm) wide and 40" (101.5cm) long

BORDER: Four strips 3" (7.5cm) wide and 40"
(101.5cm) long of each of two colors

BACKING: 20" × 20" (51 × 51cm)

BATTING: 20" × 20" (51 × 51cm)

♦ **INDIAN TRAIL (page 69)**

4" (10cm) block size

Make 16

♦ **FRAME BORDER (page 247)**

1" (2.5cm) wide

Make 2 to finish 16" (40.5cm) long

Make 2 to finish 18" (45.5cm) long with corner
pattern

MEMORY ALBUM QUILT

FINISHED SIZE: 13" × 13" (33 × 33cm)

FABRIC REQUIREMENTS:

FOND MEMORY BLOCKS: Scraps 1½" (4 cm) wide
    for small triangles (brown in photograph)

One 2½" (6.5cm) wide strip 40" (101.5cm) long for
    large triangle

One 3" (7.5cm) wide strip 40" (101.5cm) long for
    pinwheels (red in photograph)

One 2" (5cm) strip 40" (101.5cm) long for background

PICTURE FRAME BLOCKS: Scraps 1½" (4 cm) wide
    for small triangles

One strip 2½" (6.5cm) wide for frame

Two 3" (7.5cm) wide strips 40" (101.5cm) long for
    corner triangles

Five 2½" × 2½" (6.5 × 6.5cm) squares for picture
    frame center

BORDER: Four 1" × 13½" (2.5 × 34.5cm) strips

Scraps for corners

BACKING: 15" × 15" (38 × 38cm)

BATTING: 15" × 15" (38 × 38cm)

◆ **PICTURE FRAME (page 77)**

    4" (10cm) block size

    Make 5

◆ **FOND MEMORY (page 77)**

    4" (10cm) block size

    Make 4 (sixteen 2" [5cm] subunit foundations)

Use photo transfer medium to add photographs
to the fabric squares inside the picture frame blocks.

NIGHT AND DAY QUILT

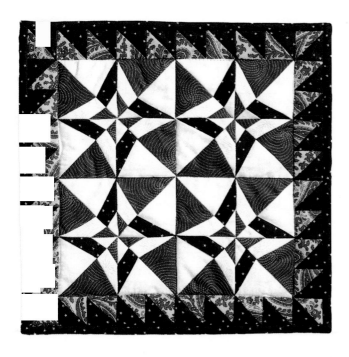

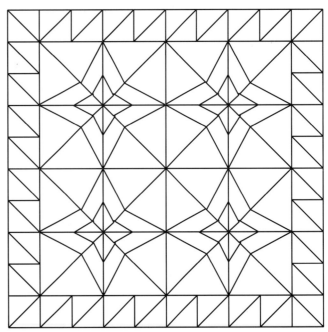

FINISHED SIZE: 10" × 10" (25.5 × 25.5cm)

FABRIC REQUIREMENTS:

BLOCKS: Strips 1½" (4cm) wide and 1½" (4cm), 2½" (6.5cm), and 3½" (9cm) long of dark and light fabrics

BORDER: Two strips 1½" (4cm) wide and 40" (101.5cm) long of dark and light fabrics

BACKING: 12" × 12" (30 × 30cm)

BATTING: 12" × 12"(30 × 30cm)

◆ **NIGHT AND DAY (page 51)**

   4" (10cm) block size

   Make 4

◆ **HALF-SQUARE TRIANGULAR BORDER (page 245)**

   1" (2.5cm) wide

Make 2 to finish 12" (30cm) long

Make 2 to finish 14" (35.5cm) long (to include corners)

This is another striking two-color quilt. For a more subtle effect, use a monochromatic theme: choose two shades of a color, such as a dark and light blue.

ORIENTAL WONDER QUILT

FINISHED SIZE: 12½" × 17" (31.5 × 43cm)

FABRIC REQUIREMENTS:

KIMONO BLOCKS: Strips 1½" (4 cm) and 2½" (6.5 cm) wide and 1½" (4 cm) wide for kimono

SAMURAI FAN BLOCKS: Scraps of six fabrics

SASHING: Three rectangles 1" × 4" (2.5 × 10cm) to join block horizontally and two rectangles 1" × 9" (2.5 × 23cm) to join vertically

BORDER: Two rectangles 2½" × 9" (6.5 × 23cm) for top and bottom borders and two rectangles 2½" × 13½" (6.5 × 34.5cm) for side borders

BACKING: 15" × 19" (38 × 48cm)

BATTING: 15" × 19" (38 × 48cm)

♦ **KIMONO (page 28)**

    4" (10cm) block size

    Make 6

♦ **SAMURAI FAN (page 29)**

    2" (5cm) block size

    Make 4

PINEBURR BEAUTY QUILT

FINISHED SIZE: 10" × 14" (25.5 × 35.5cm)

FABRIC REQUIREMENTS:

BLOCKS (in colors as shown in photograph):

One 2" (5cm) wide strip 40" (101.5cm) long

    in dark green

Two 1½" (4cm) wide strips 40" (101.5cm) long in

    light green

Two 2" (5cm) wide strips 40" (101.5cm) long in

    purple

Two 2½" (6.5cm) wide strips 40" (101.5cm) long in

    off-white (background)

BORDER: Two 2" (5cm) wide strips 40" (101.5cm)

    long of two colors

BACKING: 12" × 16" (30 × 40.5cm)

BATTING: 12" × 16" (30 × 40.5cm)

◆ **PINEBURR BEAUTY (page 36)**

    4" (10cm) block size

    Make 6 (24 2" [5cm] subunit foundations)

◆ **EQUILATERAL TRIANGLE BORDER (page 246)**

    1" (2.5cm) wide

Make 2 to finish 8" (20.5cm) long

Make 2 to finish 8" (20.5cm) long (plus corner blocks)

SPRING SONG QUILT

FINISHED SIZE: 16" × 16" (40.5 × 40.5cm)

FABRIC REQUIREMENTS:

4" (10cm) BLOCKS: One strip 3" (7.5cm) wide and 40" (101.5cm) long in red

One strip 2" (5cm) wide and 40" (101.5cm) long in green

One strip 3" (7.5cm) wide and 40" (101.5cm) long in white

2" (5cm) BLOCKS: Two strips 2" (5cm) wide and 40" (101.5cm) long in red

Two strips 2½" (6.5cm) wide and 40" (101.5cm) long in green

Two strips 2" (5cm) wide and 40" (101.5cm) long in green

BORDER AND SASHING: Three strips 3" (7.5cm) wide and 40" (101.5cm) long in red

Two strips 3" (7.5cm) wide and 40" (101.5cm) long in dark green

Three strips 3" (7.5cm) wide and 40" (101.5cm) long in light green

BACKING: 18" × 18" (45.5 × 45.5cm)

BATTING: 18" × 18" (45.5 × 45.5cm)

♦ **CROCUS (page 36)**

2" (5cm) block size

Make 20

♦ **CROCUS (page 36)**

4" (10cm) block size

Make 4

♦ **FRAME BORDER (page 247)**

2" (5cm) wide

Make 12 sashing strips in dark green and red with light green corner blocks

Make 2 borders to finish 14" (35.5cm) long and 2 to finish 16" (40.5cm) long, the latter to include the corners, following the photograph for color placement

TALL PINE TREES QUILT

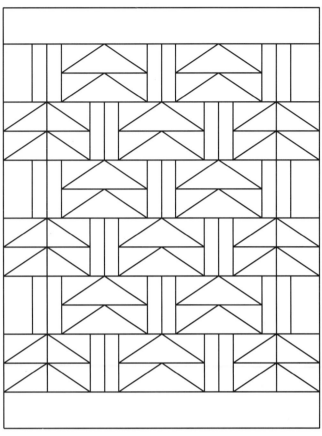

FINISHED SIZE: 11" × 14" (28 × 35.5cm)

FABRIC REQUIREMENTS:

BLOCKS: 2½" (6.5cm) wide strips in green for tree greenery

One 3" (7.5cm) wide strip 40" (101.5cm) long in brown for tree trunks

Two 2½" (6.5cm) wide strips 40" (101.5cm) long in blue for background

One 2½" (6.5cm) wide strip 40" (101.5cm) long in green for outside left and right blocks

BORDER: Two strips 1¾" × 11½" (4.5 × 29cm) each for top and bottom borders

BACKING: 13" × 16" (33 × 40.5cm)

BATTING: 13" × 16" (33 × 40.5cm)

◆ **TALL PINE TREE (page 69)**

4" (10cm) block size

Make 9

◆ **TALL PINE TREE (page 69)**

End block 4" (10cm) wide

Make 3 half-blocks

◆ **TALL PINE TREE (page 69)**

End block 4" (10cm) wide

Make 3 half-blocks (mirror image)

Block D is a 1" x ½" (2.5 x 1.25cm) strip.

Block E is the end block without piece 5. Make 6.

Make 3 mirror pieces as well.

ROSE STAR

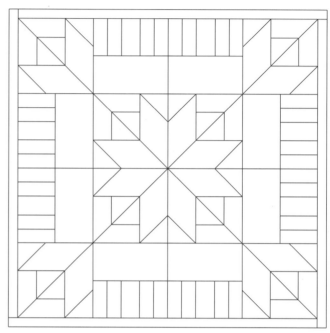

FINISHED SIZE: 17" × 17" (43 × 43cm)

FABRIC REQUIREMENTS:

BLOCKS: Scraps of fabric for pieced blocks

BORDER: 4" (10cm) strips each 1" × 17"

      (2.5 × 43cm)

BACKING: 22" × 22" (56 × 56cm)

BATTING: 21" × 21" (53.5 × 53.5cm)

♦ **CORNER BUD (page 106)**

    4" (10cm) block size

    Make 8

♦ **CHARMING GARDEN (page 96)**

    4" (10cm) block size

    Make 8

This quilt is a good choice for a beginner.

WATER GARDENS

FINISHED SIZE: 20" × 20" (51 × 51cm)

FABRIC REQUIREMENTS:

BLOCKS: Scraps of fabric for pieced blocks and
border blocks

BACKING: 24" × 24" (61 × 61cm)

BATTING: 24" × 24" (61 × 61cm)

♦ **FISH I (page 135)**

4" (10cm) block size

Make 4

♦ **FISH II (page 135)**

4" (10cm) block size

Make 8 (reverse 4)

♦ **WATER LILY (page 108)**

4" (10cm) block size

Make 4

♦ **TWISTED RIBBON BORDER (page 238)**

2" (5cm) block size

Make 2 to finish 16" (40.5cm) long

Make 2 to finish 18" (45.5cm) including corner

blocks at each end for top and bottom.

Enlarge pattern 200 percent.

GARDEN BIRDS

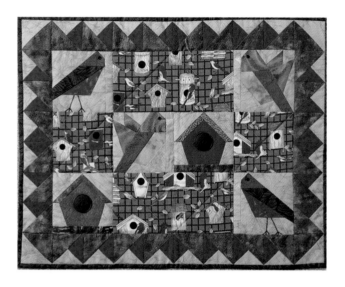

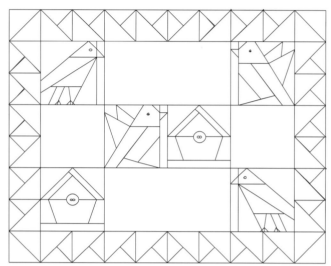

FINISHED SIZE: 16" × 20" (40.5 × 51cm)

FABRIC REQUIREMENTS:

BLOCKS: Scraps of fabric for birdhouse blocks

PLAIN SQUARES: Two 4½" × 4½" (11.5 × 11.5cm)

PLAIN RECTANGLES: Two 4½" × 8½" (11.5 × 21.5cm)

BORDER: Scraps of three fabrics cut in 3" (7.5cm) wide strips

BACKING: 20" × 24" (51 × 61cm)

BATTING: 20" × 24" (51 × 61cm)

◆ **BIRD (page 134)**

    4" (10cm) block size

    Make 2 (reverse 1)

◆ **FLYING BIRD (page 135)**

    4" (10cm) block size

    Make 2 (reverse 1)

◆ **BIRDHOUSE (page 146)**

    4" (10cm) block size

    Make 2

◆ **FENCE TOP BORDER (page 239)**

    2" (5cm) block size

Make 2 to finish 12" (30cm) long

Make 2 to finish 20" (51cm) long (including corner blocks)

Use birdhouse-theme fabric for the plain squares and rectangles.

GARDEN PLANS

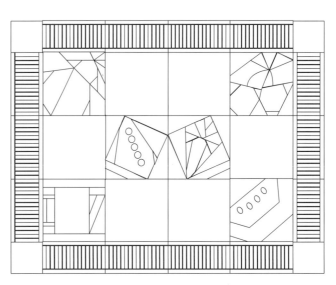

FINISHED SIZE: 16" × 20" (40.5cm × 51cm)

FABRIC REQUIREMENTS:

BLOCKS: Scraps of fabric for pieced blocks

Six 4½" (11.5cm) squares of garden theme fabric

BORDER: 3" (7.5cm) wide strips of two fabrics

Four 2½" (6.5cm) squares for corner blocks

BACKING: 20" × 24" (51 × 61cm)

BATTING: 20" × 24" (51 × 61cm)

- ◆ **PEAR (page 126)**

    4" (10cm) block size

    Make 1

- ◆ **CHERRIES (page 126)**

    4" (10cm) block size

    Make 1

- ◆ **PEA POD (page 125)**

    4" (10cm) block size

    Make 1

- ◆ **CARROT (page 125)**

    4" (10cm) block size

    Make 1

- ◆ **WATERING CAN (page 146)**

    4" (10cm) block size

    Make 1

- ◆ **LATTICE FENCE BORDER (page 240)**

    2" (5cm) block size

    Make 2 to finish 12" (30cm) long

    Make 2 to finish 20" (51cm) long (including plain

    corner blocks at each end)

The two center blocks are 2" (5cm) versions of the snap pea and carrot blocks inside seed packet blocks (page 126). Alternatively make the vegetable blocks in 4" (10cm) size.

Use garden-theme fabric for the plain squares.

GOOD MORNING SUNSHINE

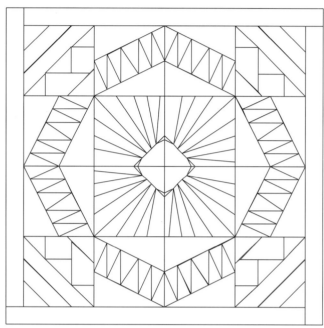

FINISHED SIZE: 18" × 18" (45.5 × 45.5cm)

FABRIC REQUIREMENTS:

BLOCKS: Scraps of fabric

BORDER: Four strips each cut 1½" × 17½"

      (4 × 45cm)

BACKING: 22" × 22" (56 × 56cm)

BATTING: 22" × 22" (56 × 56cm)

    ♦ **CORNER ROSE (page 108)**

4" (10cm) block size

Make 4

♦ **THORNY TRAIL (page 95)**

    4" (10cm) block size

    Make 8

♦ **CORNER SUNSHINE (page 158)**

    4" (10cm) block size

    Make 4

This pattern works up well as a scrap quilt of many different fabrics.

LEAFY RAMBLE

FINISHED SIZE: 24" × 24" (61 × 61cm)

FABRIC REQUIREMENTS:

BLOCKS: Scraps of fabric for pieced blocks

For small triangles cut strips 2½" (6.5cm) wide

Four 4½" × 4½" (11.5 × 11.5cm) squares for plain
      corner blocks

BORDER: Scraps of three fabrics cut in
      3" (7.5cm) wide strips

BACKING: 28" × 28" (71 × 71cm)

BATTING: 28" × 28" (71 × 71cm)

◆ **GARDEN RAMBLE (page 96)**

    4" (10cm) block size

    Make 16

◆ **LEAF BUD (page 109)**

    4" (10cm) block size

    Make 4

◆ **CACTUS FLOWER (page 107)**

    2" × 4" (5 × 10cm) block size

    Make 8

◆ **AUTUMN LEAF (page 107)**

    4" (10cm) block size

    Make 4

    Add a 4½" × 2½" (11.5 × 6.5cm) strip of fabric to
the bottom of each pieced rectangular block to make
a 4" (10cm) finished square.

PARTY LIGHTS

FINISHED SIZE: 18" × 18" (45.5 × 45.5cm)

FABRIC REQUIREMENTS:

BLOCKS: Scraps of fabric for pieced blocks

For small triangles cut strips 2½" (6.5cm) wide

Four 2½" (6.5cm) squares for corner blocks

BORDER: 4 strips each 1" × 17½" (2.5 × 45cm)

BACKING: 22" × 22" (56 × 56cm)

BATTING: 22" × 22" (56 × 56cm)

♦ **GARDEN PARTY (page 95)**

   2" × 4" (5 × 10cm) block size

   Make 8 (reverse 4)

♦ **GARDEN PATH (page 94)**

   4" (10cm) block size

   Make 4

♦ **GARDEN LIGHT (page 145)**

   4" (10cm) block size

   Make 5

♦ **JAPANESE LANTERN (page 144)**

   4" (10cm) block size

   Make 4

Design your own quilt by substituting blocks of your choice for the nine blocks in the center of the quilt.

SUMMER AFTERNOON

FINISHED SIZE: 20" × 20" (51 × 51cm)

FABRIC REQUIREMENTS:

BLOCKS: Scraps of fabric

BACKING: 24" × 24" (61 × 61cm)

BATTING: 24" × 24" (61 × 61cm)

◆ **BUTTERFLY I (page 134)**

    4" (10cm) block size

    Make 4

◆ **PICKET FENCE (page 144)**

    2" × 4" (5 × 10cm) block size

    Make 8

◆ **WHIRLIGIG (page 144)**

    4" (10cm) block size

    Make 4

◆ **FENCE TOP BORDER (page 239)**

    2" (5cm) block size

Make 2 to finish 14" (35.5cm) long for sides

FLOWER GARDEN

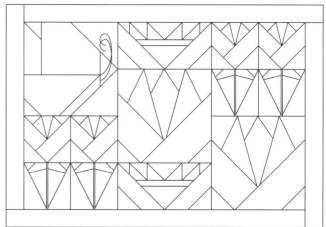

FINISHED SIZE: 13½" × 9½" (34.5 × 24cm)

FABRIC REQUIREMENTS:

BLOCKS: Scraps of fabric

BORDER: Two strips each 1¼" × 9¼"

        (3.5 × 23.5cm) for sides

Two strips each 1¼" × 13¼" (3.5 × 33.5cm) for

        top and bottom

BACKING: 18" × 14" (45.5 × 35.5cm)

BATTING: 18" × 14" (45.5 × 35.5cm)

◆ **BUTTERFLY II (page 135)**

    4" (10cm) block size

◆ **CACTUS FLOWER (page 107)**

    2" × 4" (5 × 10cm) block size

◆ **TALL FLOWER (page 106)**

    4" (10cm) block size

◆ **WATER LILY (page 108)**

    4" (10cm) block size

    Embroider the antennae or draw in with permanent marker.

TROPICAL PARADISE

FINISHED SIZE: 18" × 22" (45.5 × 56cm)

FABRIC REQUIREMENTS:

BLOCKS: Scraps of fabric

BORDER: Two strips each 1½" × 17½"

    (4 × 45cm) for sides

Two strips each 1½" × 21½" (4 × 53.5cm) for

    top and bottom

BACKING: 22" × 26" (56 × 66cm)

BATTING: 22" × 26" (56 × 66cm)

◆ **SPIKE FLOWER (page 108)**

    4" (10cm) block size

    Make 4

◆ **CLEMATIS BUD (page 106)**

    4" (10cm) block size

    Make 8

◆ **CACTUS FLOWER (page 107)**

    2" × 4" (5 × 10cm) block size

    Make 2

◆ **BELLFLOWER (page 107)**

    4" (10cm) block size

    Make 6

Add a 2½" × 4½" (4 × 11.5cm) rectangle to the

bottom of each pieced rectangular cactus flower

block to make a 4" (10cm) finished square.

WOODLANDS

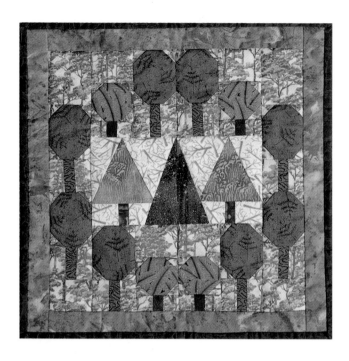

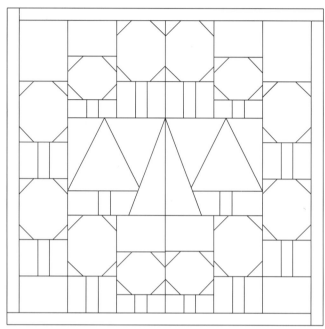

FINISHED SIZE: 14" × 14" (35.5 × 35.5cm)

FABRIC REQUIREMENTS:

BLOCKS: Scraps of fabric

Two 2½" × 3" (6.5 × 7.5cm) rectangles and four

    2" × 2½" (5 × 6.5cm) rectangles for plain blocks

BORDER: Four strips each 1½" × 13½"

    (4 × 34.5cm)

BACKING: 22" × 22" (56 × 56cm)

BATTING: 22" × 22" (56 × 56cm)

♦ **APPLE TREES (page 109)**

    Make 8 tall tree blocks

    Make 4 small tree blocks

♦ **GREEN WOODS (page 156)**

    4" (10cm) block size

    Make 2 (reverse 1)

To put the quilt top together, stitch the apple trees and plain blocks strips for the two sides. Sew the center apple trees together for top and bottom, then stitch the two sections to the green woods. Add the apple tree side strips.

MOUNTAIN SEASONS

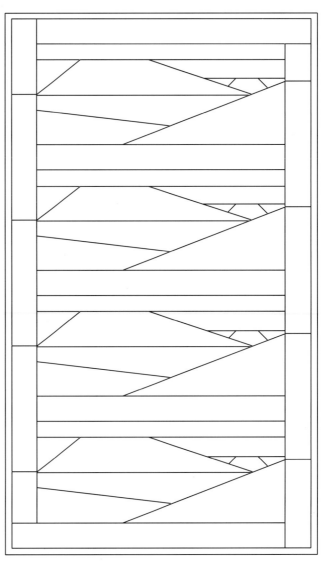

FINISHED SIZE: 12" × 21" (30.5 × 53.5cm)

FABRIC REQUIREMENTS:

BLOCKS: Scraps of fabric

BORDER: Three strips each cut 1½" × 10½"

    (4 × 26.5cm)

BACKING: 16" × 25" (40.5 × 63cm)

BATTING: 16" × 25" (40.5 × 63cm)

◆ **SUNRISE OVER MOUNTAIN LAKE (page 156)**

    Enlarge 200 percent, to 4" × 10" (10 × 25.5cm)

HEARTTHROB

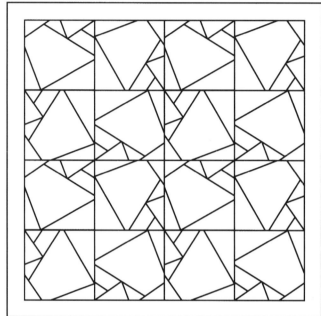

FINISHED SIZE: 24" x 24" (61 x 61cm)

FABRIC REQUIREMENTS:

BLOCKS: Large scraps of three different fabrics

INNER BORDER: Two strips 1½" x 16½"

        (4 x 42cm) and two strips 1½" x 18½"

        (4 x 47cm)

OUTER BORDER: Two strips 3½" x 18½"

        (9 x 47cm) and two strips 3½" x 24½"

        (9 x 62cm)

BACKING: 28" x 28" (71 x 71cm)

BATTING: 24" x 24" (61 x 61cm)

HEARTTHROB BLOCK (Page 184)

    4" (10cm) block size

    Make 8

PUPPY LOVE

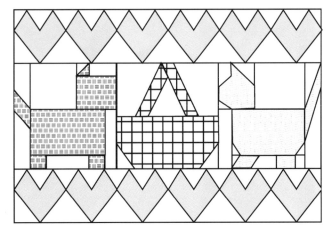

FINISHED SIZE: 8" x 26" (20.5 x 66cm)

FABRIC REQUIREMENTS:

BLOCKS: Assorted fabrics

BORDER: Five 4½" x 2½" (11.5 x 6.5cm)

      pieces to go between and to both sides of

      the blocks and two 26½" x 2½" (21 x 6.5cm)

      pieces for top and bottom border

BACKING: 12" x 30" (30.5 x 76cm)

BATTING: 12" x 30" (30.5 x 76cm)

SCOTTIE DOG BLOCK (Page 197)

    4" (10cm) block size

    Make 1

PLAYFUL KITTY BLOCK (Page 197)

    4" (10cm) block size

    Make 1

FLOWER BASKET (Page 196)

    4" (10cm) block size

    Make 1

GARDEN FLUTTER

FINISHED SIZE: 11" x 11" (28 x 28cm)

FABRIC REQUIREMENTS:

BLOCKS: Assorted fabrics

BORDER: Assorted fabrics

BACKING: 14" x 14" (35.5 x 35.5cm)

BATTING: 14" x 14" (35.5 x 35.5cm)

BINDING: 1¾" (4.5cm) wide strips

BUD AND BUTTERFLY (Page 198)

> 4" (10cm) block size
>
> Make 4
>
> Stitch 1" (2.5cm) wide solid color fabric strips to
>
> > outside edges of assembled quilt blocks.

CUPID'S DART BORDER (Page 241)

> 1" (2.5cm) wide border
>
> Make 4 (Pattern and mirror flip to make one
>
> > border.)

AFTERNOON DELIGHT

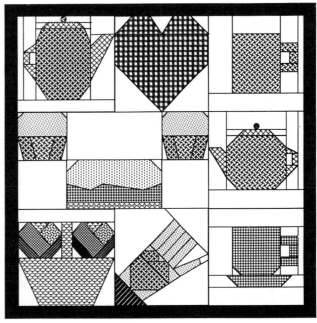

FINISHED SIZE: 13" x 13" (33 x 33cm)

FABRIC REQUIREMENTS: Scraps of fabric

BLOCKS: Two 2½" (6.5cm) squares to add to the Cupcake blocks

One 2½" x 4½" (6 x 11cm) rectangle to add to the Tea Cake block

BORDER: 1" (2.5cm) wide strips to finish ½" (1.3cm) wide

BACKING: 16" x 16" (40.5 x 40.5cm)

BATTING: 16" x 16" (40.5 x 40.5cm)

BINDING: 1¾" (4.5cm) wide strips

CUPCAKE (Page 219)
>   2" (5cm) block size
>   Make 2

COFFEE POT (Page 221)
>   4" (10cm) block size
>   Make 1

LARGE UPRIGHT HEART (Page 168)
>   4" (10cm) block size
>   Make 1

FRIENDSHIP MUG (Page 220)
>   4" (10cm) block size
>   Make 1

TEA CAKE (Page 219)
>   2" x 4" (5 x 10cm) block size
>   Make 1

TEAPOT (Page 221)
>   4" (10cm) block size
>   Make 1

BASKET OF FLOWERS (Page 199)
>   4" (10cm) block size
>   Make 1

DIAGONAL HEART IN HAND (Page 214)
>   4" (10cm) block size
>   Make 1

CUP AND SAUCER (Page 221)
>   4" (10cm) block size
>   Make 1

YOU ARE INVITED...

The greatest pleasure in creating books is meeting people who share the quilting passion. The quilting family is a melting pot of those who love the art and craft of quilting, resulting in a sisterhood that brings me, for one, immense pleasure.

In this spirit, let's have a quilting bee of sorts through the mail. Whether you use the designs in this book or any other in the series, make these ideas a springboard for your creativity, or embark on your own, I'd love to see what you're making. Send me photos of your quilts and a letter about yourself and your quilting to the address below. Or contact me via the online service below. I look forward to meeting you.

JODIE DAVIS
Jodie Davis Publishing, Inc.
15 West 26th Street
New York, NY 10010
or via e-mail: CompuServe: 73522,2430

Linda is an active teacher and lecturer, and is always interested in hearing from readers and fellow quilters. If you would like more information on her classes or need help with any of the patterns in this book, please contact her.

Linda Hampton Schiffer
(at above address)
or via e-mail : quilter@lhsdesigns.jagunet.com

SOURCES

CLOTILDE
B3000
Louisiana, MO 63353-3000
(800) 772-2891
Catalog: Free
Sewing and quilting supplies.

CONNECTING THREADS
5750 N.E. Hassalo
Portland, OR 97213
(800) 574-6454
Catalog: Free
Quilting and related books, and more.

G STREET FABRICS
11854 Rockville Pike
Rockville, MD 20852
(301) 231-8998
If you ever get a chance, do visit this incredible Washington, D.C., landmark. The selection of fabric, notions, and trims is mind-boggling. The education department offers an intriguing selection of classes. Call for special requests and to inquire about their swatch service.

KEEPSAKE QUILTING
Route 25
P.O. Box 1618
Centre Harbor, NH 03226-1618
(800) 865-9458
(603) 253-8731
Catalog: Free
Pigma pens, books, fabric, huge selection of quilting supplies.

THE QUILT FARM
P.O. Box 7877
Saint Paul, MN 55107
(800) 435-6201
Catalog: Free
Books, fabrics, patterns, and quilting supplies.

QUILTS & OTHER COMFORTS
1 Quilters Lane
P.O. Box 4100
Golden, CO 80401-0100
(800) 881-6624
Catalog: Free
Books, large selection of quilting supplies.

BIBLIOGRAPHY

Fanning, Robbie, and Tony Fanning. *The Complete Book of Machine Quilting*. 2nd edition. Radnor, Penn.: Chilton Book Company, 1994.

Fones, Marianne, and Liz Porter. *Quilter's Complete Guide*. Birmingham, Ala.: Oxmoor House, 1993.

Hargrave, Harriet. *Heirloom Machine Quilting*. Lafayette, Calif.: C&T Publishing, 1990.

McKlvey, Susan. *Friendship's Offering: Techniques and Inspiration for Writing on Quilts*. Lafayette, Calif.: C&T Publishing, 1990.

Singer Sewing Reference Library. *Quilting by Machine*. Minnetonka, Minn.: Cy DeCosse Inc., 1990.

Thomas, Donna Lynn. *A Perfect Match: A Guide to Precise Machine Piecing*. Bothell, Wash.: That Patchwork Place, 1993.

INDEX